ADVANCE PRAISE FOR

The Franciscan Saints

Pope Francis has spotlighted the poor man of Assisi just as the world careens in a direction desperately in need of a Franciscan influence. The holy witnesses highlighted in this collection contextualize the charism in other troubled times and incarnate the spirit of Clare and Francis in concrete human form. Once again, Robert Ellsberg inspires, giving a few well-worn saints a fresh coat of paint, and bringing lesser-known figures out of the shadows.

— Pat Farrell, OSF, Sister of St. Francis of Dubuque, Iowa, former LCWR president, currently serving in Honduras

I read from at least one of Robert Ellsberg's saint books every morning after my quiet sit. Now I get to read more about my own Franciscan family of saints! He is offering the world many unknown wonderful lives, inspiration from so many angles, and models of holiness in an age that no longer believes such goodness is even possible. They all tell us that it is!

— Fr. Richard Rohr, OFM, Center for Action and Contemplation, Albuquerque, New Mexico

Robert Ellsberg has made a great contribution to the Franciscan family, as well as Church and world, by telling the stories of outstanding men and women who followed in the footsteps of Francis of Assisi. In his clear crisp style, Ellsberg translates the lives of men and women into real life struggles of darkness, perseverance, and commitment. His collation of Franciscan saints confirms that holiness is not like starched linen but emerges amidst the chaos and darkness of life when God is the center of one's life. Saints are not born by nature but by grace and Ellsberg's pithy lives shows that responding to God's invitation to love is the first step toward holiness. This is a wonderful book for those interested in the demands of Gospel life. Francis and his followers continue to show us that where the heart lies so too lives the treasure.

— Ilia Delio, OSF, Josephine C. Connelly Endowed Chair in Theology, Villanova University

Finally the stories of the well-known and the unknown holy women and men of the Franciscan family are gathered together in one place! Robert Ellsberg does an excellent job narrating the inspiring, compelling and, at times, challenging legacies of these saints for a new generation.

— Daniel P. Horan, OFM, author, *Dating God: Live and Love in the Way of St. Francis*

Robert Ellsberg provides us with the stories of that great cloud of witnesses who, inspired by St. Francis, have followed the crucified and risen Lord. This volume, highly recommended, both informs the mind and nourishes the spirit.

—Lawrence S. Cunningham, the University of Notre Dame

This book is a delightful must-read, for all those seeking to deepen their spirituality as followers of Jesus Christ. Robert Ellsberg enters into the lives of the *The Franciscan Saints* with an ease of storytelling; he has the ability to draw out both the challenges of their relationship with the world and their desire to serve the Kingdom of God. Included are stories of over one hundred Franciscans, from well-known saints such as Francis of Assisi and Clare, to lesser-known holy men and women who have been influenced by the Franciscan way. Robert Ellsberg brings to life both the commonness and extraordinariness of their lives that are (in his own words) "full of evangelical zeal, humility and simplicity of life, closeness to the poor, a spirit of prayer, and a certain freedom from the cares of a world preoccupied with greatness, power, and grandiose ambitions." You won't be disappointed.

—Oblate Father Ron Rolheiser, theologian, teacher, award-winning author and president of the Oblate School of Theology in San Antonio, Texas

In a very readable, popularized style, Robert Ellsberg has created insightful and inspirational interpretations of a host of holy Franciscans. They reveal a consistent thread throughout: how the commitment to personal poverty of these women and men was invariably linked to solidarity with their contemporaries who were poor.

—Michael Crosby, OFM, speaker and award-winning author of *Finding Francis: Following Christ*

This is a precious gem of short reflections on beloved Franciscan saints and saintly brothers and sisters. A good daily reflection!

—John Michael Talbot, Christian musician, bestselling author, and founder and general minister of the Brothers and Sisters of Charity

The Franciscan Saints

ROBERT ELLSBERG

franciscan
media
Cincinnati, Ohio

Most of these pieces are adapted from material originally published by Liturgical Press in *Give Us This Day* and reprinted in *Blessed Among Us: Day by Day with Saintly Witnesses*, copyright ©2016 by Robert Ellsberg. Grateful acknowledgment is made to Liturgical Press for their cooperation with this volume. Thanks also to Crossroad Publishing for permission to adapt essays on St. Francis of Assisi and St. Clare, which originally appeared in *All Saints: Daily Reflections on Saints, Prophets, and Witnesses for Our Time*, copyright ©1997 by Robert Ellsberg. All rights reserved.

Cover design by Candle Light Studio
Book design by Mark Sullivan

LIBRARY OF CONGRESS CATALOGING-IN-PUBLICATION DATA
Names: Ellsberg, Robert, 1955- author.
Title: The Franciscan saints / Robert Ellsberg.
Description: Cincinnati : Franciscan Media, 2017.
Identifiers: LCCN 2017023212 | ISBN 9781632531940 (trade paper)
Subjects: LCSH: Christian saints—Biography. | Franciscans—Biography.
Classification: LCC BX4655.3 .E45 2017 | DDC 271/.3022 [B] —dc23 LC
record available at https://lccn.loc.gov/2017023212

ISBN 978-1-63253-194-0

Copyright ©2017, Robert Ellsberg. All rights reserved.
Published by Franciscan Media
28 W. Liberty St.
Cincinnati, OH 45202
www.FranciscanMedia.org

Printed in the United States of America.
Printed on acid-free paper.
17 18 19 20 21 5 4 3 2 1

To Monica

CONTENTS

INTRODUCTION

When the number of votes was reached making me pope, the Brazilian Cardinal Claudio Hummes came up to me and said: "Don't forget the poor." Immediately, thinking of the poor, I thought of Francis of Assisi…. Francis, the man of poverty, peace, who loves and takes care of creation, a man who gives out a sense of peace, a poor man. Oh! How I would like a church that was poor and for the poor!

—POPE FRANCIS

There have been several Franciscan popes in history, most recently Pope Clement XIV (1769–1774). He is remembered, among other things, for having suppressed the Society of Jesus. Ironically, the first Jesuit elected pope, Cardinal Jorge Bergoglio, became the first to assume the name of Francis. Some initial speculation focused on whether he had meant to invoke the great Jesuit missionary St. Francis Xavier, or perhaps St. Francis de Sales. But no, as the new pope soon made clear—his inspiration was none other than St. Francis of Assisi.

That no previous pope had ventured to take that name is unsurprising. Among the many associations conjured by the name of Francis, one of the most obvious was his utter rejection of the trappings of status, power, and importance. He called his followers the Lesser Brothers. He esteemed Lady Poverty as his spouse. He called it "perfect joy" when he was reviled or treated with contempt. Whatever one may say about the papacy, its incumbents have not typically been averse to pomp and pageantry.

Yet, as soon became clear, Pope Francis aspired to live up to the challenge posed by his name. This was reflected immediately in his choice to dispense with fancy garments and the custom-made red shoes and, more notably, in his decision to forgo the Apostolic Palace in favor of a modest room in the Vatican guesthouse. But beyond these gestures of humility, the remembrance of St. Francis implied an agenda and a program for renewal. Francis, after all, was the saint who set out to rebuild and reform the Church by evoking the example and spirit of the Poor Man, Jesus. He spurned violence and power. He reached out to members of other religions. He treated women with dignity and respect. He cherished the earth and all its creatures. He pointed to a new form of human and cosmic community, marked by love. And he did all this with such a spirit of joy and freedom as to make him a source of wonder and attraction to many of his contemporaries.

This attraction continued in the years that followed his death in 1226. And it continues still. Nearly eight hundred years later, St. Francis undoubtedly remains the world's most popular saint—honored in every land, even by the secular-minded and people of other faiths. This reflects, in part, his winsome qualities and the romantic gestures that sometimes encourage sentimentality. But beneath all that, St. Francis stands as one who made the way of Jesus credible and concrete, both for those called to formal religious life and for men and women living in the ordinary world.

Jesus left no formal religious rule for his followers. The closest he came was his proclamation of the Beatitudes: Blessed are the poor in spirit, the meek, the merciful, the peacemakers…. Francis took to heart this spiritual vision and translated it into a way of life. In various ways, other saints before and since have done the same. But for many men and women since the time of Francis, his particular example has offered a distinctive key to the Gospel—or, as Pope Francis might say, "a new way of seeing and interpreting reality." Among the central features of this key: the vision of a Church that is "poor and for the poor"; a resolve to take seriously Jesus's example of self-emptying love; the way of mercy and compassion; above all, a determination to proclaim the Gospel not only with words but with one's life.

The first followers of Francis joined him in walking into the unknown, improvising as they went along. Later, that path became more regularized and even institutionalized. Within years of the founder's death, his order was buffeted between factions divided over how literally to adhere to the Poverello's extreme ideal of poverty. There were those who leaned toward greater structure and discipline, while others favored Francis's more spontaneous, charismatic style. Yet for all the diversity within the broad Franciscan movement, the figure of St. Francis remained the essential touchstone and guide.

In this book, I have selected more than a hundred Franciscans — many, but not all, drawn from the long list of official Franciscan saints. Beginning with the founders, Francis and Clare and their first generation of followers, they include friars, women religious, and the diverse family of tertiary or Third Order Franciscans, a company comprised of laypeople, clergy, and even popes. As the original Franciscan message spread like wildfire through the kingdoms of Europe, many of the early followers were sons and daughters of royalty, suddenly moved to renounce their power and privilege. There followed preachers and penitents, hermits and vagabonds, poets, theologians, missionaries and martyrs. Some of them lived in organized religious communities. Others were immersed in the world of family, work, and secular life. And yet they are linked by a family resemblance. Among the notable features: evangelical zeal, humility and simplicity of life, closeness to the poor, a spirit of prayer, and a certain freedom from the cares of a world preoccupied with greatness, power, and grandiose ambitions.

Clearly, the influence of St. Francis extends beyond the company of his avowed followers. His life has inspired numerous novels, films, and works of art. There are movements with no official Franciscan connection, which yet bear the spirit of St. Francis. One thinks of the Catholic Worker, founded by Dorothy Day and Peter Maurin, which embraces a radical spirit of voluntary poverty, while engaging in works of mercy and the witness for peace. Or the Community of Sant'Egidio in Rome, which promotes the cause of reconciliation, engages in service to the homeless and those with AIDS, and campaigns against the death penalty. In those who promote the cause of interreligious dialogue, who show care for creation, who remember the poor and respond with mercy and compassion, we can see the true spirit of St. Francis. Insofar as Pope Francis has embraced these concerns, one can say that he has truly recalled the vision of St. Francis in our time.

In different ways, and under various circumstances, that vision was felt by all the men and women whose stories follow. In one way or another they were all struck by the question that came to St. Ignatius of Loyola, the founder of the Jesuits, whose dramatic conversion was prompted by his meditation on the saints: "What if I should do as St. Francis did?" Another translation of that question might be: What if I were to live as if the Gospel were true? As Carlo Carretto, a modern admirer, has observed: "At least once in our lives we have dreamed of becoming saints.… Stumbling under the weight of the contradictions of our lives, for a fleeting moment, we glimpsed the possibility of building within ourselves a place of simplicity and light.… This is when St. Francis entered our lives in some way."

Thus, St. Francis entered the lives of the saints and witnesses remembered in this book. What dreams may follow from remembering their stories is the subject of another book.

St. Francis of Assisi
Founder of the Friars Minor
(CA. 1182–1226)
. . . .

St. Francis was born in the Umbrian city of Assisi about the year 1182. His parents were Pietro di Bernardone, a wealthy cloth merchant, and his French-born wife, Pica. Francis was one of the privileged young men of Assisi, attracted to adventure and frivolity as well as tales of romance. He passed his time among his friends, carousing and writing songs. When he was about twenty, he donned a knight's armor and went off, filled with dreams of glory, to join a war with the neighboring city-state of Perugia. But the face of war—up close—was far from glorious. After surviving the carnage, and several additional months as a prisoner of war, he returned home, sick and broken. In the place of his previous gaiety he felt only a desperate emptiness, a feeling that there must be more to life than the success his parents envisioned for him. He took to wandering the outskirts of town, where for the first time he noticed the poor and the sick and the squalor in which they lived. What he saw repulsed him.

Francis had always been a fastidious person, keenly alert to beauty and appalled by ugliness. But then one day, as he was out riding, he came upon a leper by the side of the road. The poor man's face was horribly deformed, and he stank of disease.

Nevertheless, Francis dismounted and, still careful to remain at arm's length, offered him a few coins. Then, moved by some divine impulse, he bent down and kissed the poor man's ravaged hands. It was a turning point. From that encounter Francis's life began to take shape around an utterly new agenda, contrary to the values of his family and the world. In kissing the leper, he was not only dispensing with his fear of death and disease, but letting go of a whole identity based on status, security, and worldly success.

While praying before a crucifix in the dilapidated chapel of San Damiano, Francis heard a voice speak to him: "Francis, repair my church, which has fallen into disrepair, as you can see." At first inclined to take this assignment literally, he set about physically restoring the ruined building. Only later did he understand his mission in a wider, more spiritual sense. His vocation was to recall the Church to the radical simplicity of the Gospel, to the spirit of poverty, and the image of Christ in his poor.

To pay for his program of church repair, Francis took to divesting his father's warehouse. Pietro di Bernardone, understandably enraged, had his son arrested and brought to trial before the bishop in the public marketplace. Francis admitted his fault and restored his father's money. And then, in an extraordinary gesture, he stripped off his rich garments and handed them also to his sorrowing father, saying, "Hitherto I have called you father on earth; but now I say, 'Our Father, who art in heaven.'" The bishop hastily covered him with his own cloak, but the transformation was accomplished. Francis had become the *Poverello*, the little poor man.

The spectacle that Francis presented—the rich boy who now camped out in the open air, serving the sick, working with his hands, and bearing witness to the Gospel—attracted ridicule from the respectable citizens of Assisi. But, gradually, it held a subversive appeal. Before long a dozen other young men had joined him. Renouncing their property and their family ties, they flocked to Francis, becoming before long the nucleus of a new religious order, the Friars Minor.

The little community continued to grow. Francis and his companions lived outdoors or in primitive shelters. They worked alongside peasants in the fields in exchange for their daily bread. When there was no work, they begged or went hungry. Otherwise, they tended the sick, comforted the sorrowful, and preached the Gospel to those who would listen, an audience, in the case of Francis, that extended to flocks of birds as well as other creatures.

What was the appeal? Even his follower Brother Masseo asked this question, only half in jest: "Why you? Why does all the world seem to be running after you, and everyone seems to want to see you and hear you and obey you? You are not a handsome man. You do not have great learning or wisdom. You are not a nobleman. So why is all the world running after you?"

Francis, with characteristic humility, explained that God's glory shone all the brighter for the weakness of such an obviously "miserable servant." Nevertheless, at least part of the answer had to do with his evident authenticity. Those who encountered Francis could no longer maintain that Christ's teachings were wonderful in theory but impossible to put into practice. Even the worldly Pope Innocent III felt compelled to endorse the new order. "This man merely wishes us to live according to the Gospel. Now if we tell him that this surpasses human strength, then we are declaring that it is impossible to follow the Gospel, and blaspheming Christ, the author of the Gospel."

There was more. The example of Francis was not simply edifying but also deeply appealing. He exuded a spirit of freedom and joy. People *wanted* to be near him, to discover for themselves the secret of his joy. As Thomas of Celano, his first biographer, described him, "O how beautiful, how splendid, how glorious did he appear in the innocence of his life, in the simplicity of his words, in the purity of his heart, his love for God, in his fraternal charity, in his ardent obedience, in his peaceful submission, in his angelic countenance!" Here was a man who had evidently discovered the way to heaven. Others were eager to follow.

Francis left relatively few writings, but his life—literally the embodiment of his message—gave rise to numerous legends and parables. Many of them reflect the joy and freedom that became hallmarks of his spirituality, along with his constant tendency to turn the values of the world on their head. Where others saw security, he saw only captivity; what for others represented success was for him a source of strife, an "obstacle to the love of God and one's neighbor." He esteemed Sister Poverty as his wife, "the fairest bride in the whole world." He encouraged his brothers to welcome ridicule and persecution as a means of conforming to the folly of the cross. He taught that unmerited suffering borne patiently for love of Christ was the path to "perfect joy."

But behind such holy "foolishness" Francis could not disguise the serious challenge he posed to the Church and the society of his time. Centuries before the expression became common in the Church, Francis represented a "preferential option for the poor." Even in Francis's lifetime, the Franciscans themselves were divided about how literally to accept his call to radical material poverty. In an age of crusades and other expressions of "sacred violence," Francis also espoused a radical commitment to nonviolence. He rejected all violence as an offense against the Gospel commandment of love and a desecration of God's image in all human beings.

Francis had a vivid sense of the sacramentality of creation. All things, whether living or inanimate, reflected their Creator's love and were thus due reverence and wonder. In this spirit, he composed his famous "Canticle of the Creatures," singing the praises of Brother Sun, Sister Moon, and even Sister Death. (Significantly, Pope Francis chose the opening words of this canticle for the title of his historic encyclical on ecology: *Laudato Si': On Care for Our Common Home.*) His gratefulness exceeded his powers of description. Addressing his Creator, he wrote: "You are love, charity; You are wisdom, You are humility, You are patience. You are beauty, You are meekness, You are security, You are inner peace. You are joy, You are our hope and joy.... Great and wonderful Lord, All-powerful God, Merciful Savior."

Altogether his life and his relationship with the world — including animals, the elements, the poor and sick, women as well as men, princes, prelates, and even the sultan of Egypt, represented the breakthrough of a new model of human and cosmic community.

But ultimately, Francis attempted to do no more than to live out the teachings of Christ and the spirit of the Gospel. His identification with Christ was so intense that in 1224, while praying in his hermitage, he received the "stigmata," the physical marks of Christ's passion, on his hands and feet. His last years were marked at once by excruciating physical suffering and spiritual joy. "Welcome, Sister Death!" he exclaimed at last. At his request, he was laid naked on the bare ground. As the friars gathered around him, he gave each his blessing in turn: "I have done my part," he said. "May Christ teach you to do yours."

Francis died on October 3, 1226. He was canonized only two years later. His feast day is observed on October 4.

We have no right to glory in ourselves because of any extraordinary gifts, since these do not belong to us but to God. But we may glory in crosses, afflictions, and tribulations, because these are our own.

—St. Francis of Assisi

꧁ ♔ ꧂

St. Clare

Founder of the Poor Clares

(1194–1253)

· · · · · · · · · ·

The story of St. Clare of Assisi is inevitably linked with St. Francis, the one she called her Father, Planter, and Helper in the Service of Christ. It was Francis who gave her a vision and enabled her to define a way of life apart from the options offered her by society. But her goal in life was not to be a reflection of Francis but to be, like him, a reflection of Christ. "Christ is the way," she said, "and Francis showed it to me."

Like Francis, Clare belonged to one of the wealthy families of Assisi. Like everyone else in the town, she was aware of the remarkable spectacle that Francis had made in abandoning his respectable family and assuming the poverty of a beggar. Doubtless there were those in Assisi who respected Francis as a faithful Christian, just as there were others who believed he was a misguided fool. It was bad enough that a man of his background was tramping about the countryside, repairing abandoned churches with his bare hands and ministering to the poor and sick. But within a few years, he had begun attracting some of the most distinguished young men of the town to follow him in his brotherhood.

What Clare's family thought of all this is not known. But we know what impact it had on Clare. She heard Francis deliver a series of Lenten sermons in 1212, when she was eighteen. She arranged in stealth to meet with Francis and asked his help that she too might live "after the manner of the holy Gospel." On the evening of Palm Sunday, while her family and all the town slept, she crept out a back door, slipped through the gates of Assisi, and made her way through the dark fields and olive groves to a rendezvous with Francis and his brothers at the chapel of St. Mary of the Angels, Before the altar, she put off her fine clothes and assumed a penitential habit, while Francis sheared off her long hair as a sign of her espousal to Christ.

It is tempting to read into this episode the romance of a spiritual elopement. To understand Clare, however we must realize that it was not Francis whom she rushed to meet in the night. He provided the meeting place, but her assignation was with Christ.

Yet after Clare had taken the plunge of rejecting her family and her social station, it was not clear what the next step should be. Apparently neither Clare nor Francis had considered that far ahead. Although she wished to identify with Francis's community, it was not seemly that she should live with the brothers. Francis arranged for her to spend the night in a nearby Benedictine convent.

Her family and a company of angry suitors tracked her down some days later in Holy Week. When pleading proved fruitless, they laid hands on her and tried to drag her out by force. She finally stopped them short by tearing off her veil and revealing her shorn head. They were too late. She was already "one of them."

Francis had long intended that a community of women, corresponding to his fraternity, should be established. In Clare he had found the partner he was seeking. She was easily persuaded to found a women's community, which was established at San Damiano. It required considerably more effort by Francis to persuade her to serve as abbess. Nevertheless, Clare quickly attracted other women. Over time, these included a number of her personal relatives, including her sister Catherine and even her widowed mother. Within her lifetime, additional communities were established elsewhere in Italy, France, and Germany. Among her surviving writings are a series of moving letters to St. Agnes of Prague, a young princess who joined the movement and became one of Clare's most beloved daughters.

Unlike the friars, the Poor Ladies, as they were originally known, lived within an enclosure. But Clare shared Francis's passionate commitment to "Lady Poverty." For her this meant literal poverty and insecurity—not the luxurious "spiritual poverty" enjoyed by so many other convents, richly supported by gifts and endowments. To defend this "privilege of poverty," Clare waged a continuous struggle against solicitous prelates who tried to mitigate her austerity. This was the centerpiece of the rule she devised for her community. When the pope offered to absolve her from her rigorous vow of poverty, she answered, "Absolve me from my sins, Holy Father, but not from my wish to follow Christ." Two days before her death in 1253, she enjoyed the grace of receiving from Rome a copy of her rule embellished with the approving seal of Pope Innocent IV. A notation on the original document notes that Clare, in tearful joy, covered the parchment with kisses.

It has been said that of all the followers of Francis, Clare was the most faithful. Many stories reflect the loving bonds of friendship between them and the trust that Francis placed in her wisdom and counsel. According to one story, Francis put the question to Clare whether he should preach or devote himself to prayer. It was Clare who urged him to go into the world: "God did not call you for yourself alone but also for the salvation of others." When Francis received the stigmata, Clare thoughtfully made him soft slippers to cover his wounded feet. During a period of dejection, Francis camped out in a hut outside the convent at San Damiano. It was there that he composed the "Canticle of the Creatures," his exultant hymn to the universe.

Finally, as Francis felt the approach of Sister Death, Clare too became seriously ill. She suffered terribly at the thought that they would not meet again in this life. Francis sent word that she should put aside all grief for she *would* surely see him again before her death. And so the promise was fulfilled, though not as she had wished. After Francis's death, the brothers carried his body to San Damiano for the sisters to say their goodbyes. Thomas of Celano records that at the sight of Francis's poor and lifeless body, Clare was "filled with grief and wept aloud."

Francis was canonized a mere two years later. Clare lived on for another twenty-seven years. In her own final "Testament," written near the end of her life, Clare makes only a discrete reference to the pain of their separation and what it meant to her: "We take note…of the frailty which we feared in ourselves after the death of our holy Father Francis. He was our pillar of strength and, after God, our one consolation and support. Thus time and again, we bound ourselves to our Lady, most Holy Poverty."

As she lay dying at San Damiano, Clare offered her final blessing to the daughters gathered beside her: "May the Lord bless you and keep you. May He show his face to you and be merciful to you. May He turn his countenance to you and give you peace."

St. Clare died on August 11, 1253. She was canonized in 1255.

Place your mind before the mirror of eternity!
Place your soul in the brilliance of glory!
Place your heart in the figure of the divine substance!
And transform your whole being into the image
of the Godhead Itself through contemplation!

—St. Clare of Assisi

⚜

St. Berard and Companions
Martyrs
(1220)
· · · · ·

In 1219, in the midst of the Fifth Crusade, St. Francis embarked on a risky mission. Crossing the battlefield in Syria he sought an audience with the Sultan Malik al-Kamil of Egypt. Though he did not succeed in converting the sultan, he was received graciously and permitted to return without harm. A different fate awaited five Franciscans who set out the next year to preach to the Muslims. Brother Berard, who spoke Arabic, along with Brothers Peter, Odo, Accursio, and Adjutus, first tried to preach to the Moors in Seville. When they were banished, they sailed for Morocco.

Upon arriving on the North African shore, they immediately began to preach in the public square, where they were regarded as lunatics and promptly arrested. Brought before the sultan in Marrakesh, they refused an ultimatum to depart or to keep silent, whereupon the sultan drew his scimitar and beheaded them each in turn.

The remains of these friars—the first Franciscan martyrs— were returned to Italy in a solemn journey. Among those deeply affected along the route was an Augustinian canon in Portugal, later known as St. Anthony of Padua, who was inspired by their example to become a Franciscan.

St. Berard and his companions were canonized in 1481.

Now I can truly say that I have five Friars Minor.

—St. Francis,
on hearing news of the martyrs' deaths

ᘒᕈᘔ

ST. ANTHONY OF PADUA

Franciscan Friar, Doctor of the Church

(1195–1231)
· · · · · · · · · ·

St. Anthony, who was born in Lisbon, first entered religious life as an Augustinian canon in Coimbra. There one day he met a group of visiting Franciscans (St. Berard and his companions) on their way to Morocco. He was greatly impressed by these courageous missionaries, the more so when news came of their subsequent martyrdom, followed by the return of their remains by way of his monastery. At once, he was inspired to join the Franciscans. He was accepted and was even granted his wish to follow in the footsteps of the martyrs. But no sooner had he arrived in Morocco than he became so ill that he was forced to turn around.

In 1221, he attended—along with three thousand other friars—a great Franciscan gathering, the last held in the lifetime of St. Francis. Afterward, he received a lowly assignment to a small hospice for lay brothers at Monte Paolo.

But soon his star would shine. At an important occasion, where the preacher failed to arrive, Anthony was asked to extemporize. He astonished his audience with the unexpected elegance, conviction, and profound learning of his sermon. Word quickly spread, and Anthony received a letter from Francis himself authorizing him to preach and to teach theology to the friars.

Eventually, he was sent on a preaching mission that covered all of Italy. Thousands flocked to hear his open-air sermons, and his visits had the impact of a spiritual revival. He attacked the tyranny of the powerful, exhorting his listeners to compassion and charity toward the poor, and he was unsparing when it came to the failings of the clergy and worldly bishops, whom he called "the most impudent dogs, having a harlot's forehead, refusing to blush." So successful were his exhortations to charity that he earned the title "Friend of the Poor."

Anthony died on June 13, 1231, at the age of thirty-six. He was buried in Padua, where he had spent his last years, and his canonization followed only a year later. In 1946, Pope Pius XII declared him a Doctor of the Church. (Popularly, he is often invoked for his help in locating lost objects.)

༄ ༅ ༄

Attribute to God every good that you have received. If you take credit for something that does not belong to you, you will be guilty of theft.

— St. Anthony of Padua

⚜

ST. ELIZABETH OF HUNGARY
Princess, Third Order Franciscan
(1207–1231)
. . . .

St. Elizabeth, the daughter of Hungarian royalty, was betrothed at the age of four to Ludwig, the nine-year-old prince of Thuringia in southern Germany. Despite the arrangement, in which they had no say, the two children established a close friendship that eventually blossomed into a loving marriage. Elizabeth bore three children. But Ludwig's family disapproved of her piety and especially her "inordinate" charity toward the poor and sick. The young princess, it was said, dressed too simply; she was too profligate in her almsgiving. After Elizabeth established several hospitals she aroused scandal by nursing the sick, even lepers, with her own hands.

Nevertheless, her instinctive spirit of poverty was only magnified upon the arrival of the first Franciscan missionaries in Germany. Elizabeth was captivated by the story of Clare and Francis (from whom she received the gift of his cloak), and she eventually embraced the rule of a Franciscan tertiary. During a time of famine, while Ludwig was away, she opened the royal granaries, thus winning the people's devotion. Such generosity, however, only increased the scorn of elite members of the court.

In 1227, Ludwig died on his way home from a crusade. In a paroxysm of grief, Elizabeth cried out, "The world is dead to me, and all that was joyous in the world." Without her husband's protection, she was at the mercy of her in-laws. They banished her from the court, forcing her to leave the palace on a wintry night, carrying nothing but her newborn child. She who had embraced the spirit of poverty now found herself happy to accept shelter in a pig shed.

Eventually, to avoid scandal, she was provided with a simple cottage, where she supported herself by spinning and fishing. She continued to visit the sick in their homes or in the hospices she had endowed. Over time, her reputation for holiness spread, and she earned the grudging respect of those who had persecuted her. In 1231, she fell ill and announced calmly that she would not recover. She died on November 17 at the age of twenty-four. She was canonized less than four years later.

We must give God what we have, gladly and with joy.

—St. Elizabeth of Hungary

᎐᎔᎐

SERVANT OF GOD BERNARD OF QUINTAVALLE

First Companion of St. Francis

(D. CA. 1241)

· · · · · · · · · ·

Bernard, one of the wealthiest young men of Assisi, became intrigued by reports about one of his peers— Francesco di Bernardone, previously known as something of a dandy and carouser—who had recently aroused wonder, as well as ridicule, by his ostentatious embrace of poverty. His curiosity piqued, Bernard invited Francis to dine with him and spend the night in his home. During the course of the night, he was so moved by the sound of his guest's ardent prayers that he confronted Francis the next day and asked his help in discerning God's will. Opening the missal at random, Francis alighted on the text, "If you wish to be perfect, go and sell all you own, and give it to the poor." A second time he opened the book and found, "Take nothing for your journey." On a third attempt, he found, "If anyone would follow me, let him deny himself." "This is the advice that the Lord has given us," Francis proclaimed. "Go and do as you have heard." Taking these instructions to heart, Bernard disposed of his property and adopted Francis's way of life.

Becoming one of Francis's most trusted companions, Bernard accompanied him on many journeys. He established a house in Bologna and undertook a special mission to the shrine at

Santiago de Compostela. When Francis was on his deathbed in 1226, "like the patriarch Jacob, with his devoted sons standing around him, grieving and weeping over the departure of so beloved a father," he asked, "Where is my firstborn son?" Placing his hand on Bernard, he bestowed a special blessing, and enjoined him to "be the head of all your Brothers."

Bernard himself died around 1241 and was buried near his spiritual father in the Basilica of St. Francis. His last words were, "I find this in my soul: not for a thousand worlds equal to this one would I want not to have served Our Lord Jesus Christ…. My dearest brothers, I beg you to love one another."

᠍᠍᠍᠍᠍᠍᠍᠍᠍᠍᠍᠍᠍᠍ᜦᜢᜦ

Of Bernard, St. Francis said that he was worthy of all reverence, and that he had founded this Order, because he was the first who had left the world, keeping back nothing for himself, but giving everything to Christ's poor.

—FROM *The Little Flowers of St. Francis*

‹❦›

BLESSED VERDIANA
Anchoress, Third Order Franciscan
(1182–1242)

· · · · · · · · · ·

Verdiana served as a housekeeper for rich relatives in Castelfiorentino, a town outside Florence. With the permission of her employers she joined a pilgrimage to the shrine of St. James at Compostela in Spain. During the course of this journey, she made such a tremendous impression on her fellow pilgrims that they begged her to remain among them. She agreed on the condition that she might live as a hermit. Gladly, they built her a small cell attached to the wall of St. Antony's oratory. There, at the age of twenty-six, following a solemn procession that included her confessor and a large crowd, she entered her cell, and allowed the entrance to be sealed behind her. In this room, with only a small window opening onto the oratory, she spent the following thirty-four years of her life.

Many people came to seek her prayers and spiritual counsel. The story circulated that Verdiana was joined in her cell by two snakes, which ate from her bowl. She also received human visitors, among them, apparently, St. Francis of Assisi, who is said to have admitted her to his Third Order.

When Verdiana died on February 10, 1242, the bells of Castelfiorentino spontaneously rang. Her cell became a famous site of pilgrimage. Her feast is observed by the Franciscans on February 16.

She had a very great love for the poor, to whom she gave everything which the piety of visitors brought to her, and she only cared to receive the poor and the afflicted.

—*Butler's Lives of the Saints*

⁂

BLESSED HUMILIANA OF CERCHI
Third Order Franciscan
(1219–1246)
· · · · · · · · ·

Humiliana was born in Florence to a noble family. Against her wishes, when she was sixteen, she was compelled by her father to marry a local nobleman. She subsequently bore three children, but it was an unhappy match. Her husband, who made his fortune through usury, treated her with disdain. She exacted private satisfaction through her acts of clandestine charity. When, five years after their marriage, her husband fell ill and died, Humiliana announced her wish to devote herself, body and soul, to Christ. Ceding her husband's fortune to his family, she requested only that they compensate all those he had defrauded.

Though she moved back to her father's home, she chafed against the constant pressure on her to remarry. "Why do you torture me every day for a husband?" she demanded. "Bring me the one to whom you wish to hand me over, and on the other side, allow me to build a furnace, so that in the meantime, I shall choose in which of the two places I wish to be placed." Defiantly, she put on the habit of a Franciscan tertiary—becoming the first in Florence—and retired to a tower on her family's property. This became her cell, which she left only to go to church, to care for the sick, or to beg alms for the Poor Clares.

She died on May 19, 1246, at the age of twenty-seven.

Lord, you knew that, to the extent that I could, I have given to you with great generosity; now, deprived of my means, I entrust to you all of my soul and body.

—BLESSED HUMILIANA OF CERCHI

St. Rose of Viterbo
Mystic, Third Order Franciscan
(1235–1252)
· · · · · · · · ·

The short life of St. Rose was set against the background of turbulent ecclesial and political conflicts in which, even as a child, she played a significant role. From her earliest years she had displayed remarkable spiritual gifts, including, at the age of nine, a vision of Our Lady, who instructed her to enter the Third Order of St. Francis.

In 1247, Rose's hometown of Viterbo was occupied by the forces of Emperor Frederick II, who was attempting to conquer the Papal States. Though only twelve, Rose took to the streets. Dressed in the simple tunic of the Third Order and carrying a crucifix, she called on growing crowds to defend the pope and to rise up and expel the usurpers. Not surprisingly, her actions incurred the wrath of the imperial party. Though denounced as an enemy of the emperor, she escaped the punishment of death. Instead, she and her parents were merely banished. Rose responded by prophesying—correctly, as it turned out—the emperor's imminent death. When, after a matter of weeks, this prophecy was fulfilled, the papal party was restored to power and Rose and her family were able to return home.

Rose spent her remaining years in prayer and seclusion in her parents' home. Though she wished to enter the Poor Clares, she was turned away for lack of a dowry.

She died in March 1252 at the age of seventeen; she was canonized in 1457.

If Jesus could be beaten for me, I can be beaten for Him. I do what He has told me to do, and I must not disobey Him.

—St. Rose of Viterbo

⬡⬢⬡

St. Agnes of Assisi
Poor Clare
(1197–1253)
. . . .

The conversion of Francesco di Bernardone, the son of a wealthy merchant, was a subject of much comment in the town of Assisi. This only increased as a procession of other prominent young men joined him in renouncing the world and embracing radical poverty. Soon they were followed by Clare, daughter of another wealthy family of Assisi. Stealing from home, she put off her fine clothes and cut off her long hair as a sign of her espousal to Christ. Francis welcomed her as the founder of a female branch of the Franciscan family, ultimately known as the Poor Clares. One of the first to join Clare was her younger sister Catherine, whom Francis renamed Agnes.

The family of the two sisters tried to compel their return, even employing armed men to carry them away by force. But these efforts were in vain; the two young women were adamant, and their parents finally relented. Francis set them up in a chapel in San Damiano, which became their convent. Agnes went on to become the abbess of a new convent in Florence, from which she wrote a touching letter to Clare and her sisters, describing the immense suffering "in body and soul" caused by her separation. This letter, the only surviving text from Agnes, describes her flood of tears and begs Clare to sympathize and mourn with her "so that you may never suffer such things and see whether there is any suffering like my suffering." After surviving this ordeal, she went on to establish new communities in Mantua, Venice, and Padua.

In August 1253, Agnes was summoned to San Damiano to be with Clare in her dying hours. As she had noted in her previous letter, Agnes had always believed "our life and death would be one, just as our manner of life in heaven would be one." Now Clare predicted that Agnes would soon follow her in death, as indeed she did. Clare died on August 11; Agnes followed on November 16. Their bodies eventually rested in adjacent tombs in the church of Santa Chiara in Assisi.

Oh sweetest mother and lady, what shall I do, what shall I say, since I do not hope to see you and my sisters again in the body. Oh, if I could express the thought in my mind as I might wish! Oh, if could open to you on this page the long sorrow I expect, which is always before me! My mind burns within and is tortured by infinite tribulations and fires. My heart moans within and my eyes do not stop pouring out rivers of tears. I am filled with sadness and without spirit I am altogether wasted away.

—St. Agnes to her sister St. Clare

SERVANT OF GOD BROTHER JUNIPER

Early Franciscan Friar

(D. 1258)

· · · · · · ·

Brother Juniper was one of the original companions of St. Francis and "a man of such unshakeable humility, patience, and self-contempt, that the rising waves of temptation and tribulation could not move him." Brother Juniper evidently attained such a degree of holiness that he was quite indifferent to the opinion or regard of others. This was fortunate, since "he was considered stupid and foolish by those who did not know how perfect he was."

Apart from the stories in his brief "Life," little is known of his biography. In these stories, he appears to function as a kind of living parable. Francis and his followers were regarded by the world as "fools for Christ." Just so, the exasperating foolishness of Juniper served among the friars as a standard by which to measure their own compromise with the wisdom of the world.

Over and over again, Juniper tested the patience of his brothers. And not infrequently, after one of his escapades, "the friars were very much shocked and scandalized, and they rebuked him forcefully, calling him a lunatic and a fool and a disgrace to the order of St. Francis, and declaring that he should be put in chains as a madman." At the sight of the poor, for instance, he was filled with such compassion that he would hand them his garments or rip off a sleeve or a cowl to give them. Not content with giving away his own habit, he would freely dispense with books, altar vestments, or anything else he could lay his hands on. As a result, "when poor people came to Brother Juniper to beg, the friars used to take and hide the things they wanted to keep."

One time, he set out to surprise the brothers by preparing a feast. After filling pots with water, he tossed in everything — "chickens with feathers and eggs in shells" — so that everything could cook together. When he set down before the friars "that hodgepodge of his, which not a single hog in the city of Rome would have eaten," they scolded him severely. Juniper displayed such humble abasement that the guardian was moved. Such an edifying example of simplicity, he said, was worth the waste of food.

So on this, and many other occasions, Juniper's foolishness ultimately bore such a lesson in charity, faith, or humility, that Francis himself was moved to observe on one occasion, "My Brothers, if only I had a great forest of such junipers."

He died in Rome in 1258.

☙ ✿ ❧

Once when Brother Juniper was praying — and perhaps he was thinking of something extraordinary — a hand appeared to him in the air, and he heard a voice saying to him: "Oh Brother Juniper, without this hand you can do nothing."

He quickly arose and ran through the friary, gazing up at heaven, dancing and shouting in a loud voice: "Indeed that is true, Lord! Indeed that is true!" And he kept on shouting that for a long time.

—FROM *The Life of Brother Juniper*

❧ ✛ ❧

BLESSED LUCHESIO AND BUONADONNA
First Members of the Third Order
(D. 1260)
· · · · · · ·

This married couple lived in the Italian town of Poggibonsi, where Luchesio worked as a merchant and moneylender. His life was marked by no special motive beyond making money. Sometime in his thirties, however, a change came over him, prompted perhaps by the death of his children. He gave up his business and distributed his wealth, keeping only a small plot of land to farm. He and his wife, Buonadonna, began to serve the sick and poor, sharing their food with those less fortunate and entrusting themselves to Providence.

At this point, St. Francis of Assisi happened to visit their town on one of his preaching tours. The couple were taken by his message and asked if there was not some way for them to follow his path without separating and entering religious life. Francis had longed to establish a Third Order in the Franciscan family for laypeople living in the world. Happily, he clothed Luchesio and Buonadonna in the plain habit and cord of the order. Tradition remembers them as the first Franciscan tertiaries.

The couple lived on for many years. As Luchesio approached the end of his life, Buonadonna prayed that they might not be separated by death. Her prayer was answered; both husband and wife died on the same day, April 28, 1260.

Luchesio was later officially beatified; Buonadonna was also remembered, at least locally, as blessed.

Implore God, who gave us to each other as companions in life, to permit us also to die together.

—BLESSED BUONADONNA

St. Jutta

Widow, Third Order Franciscan

(CA. 1200–1260)

· · · · · · · · · · · ·

St. Jutta was born in Thuringia, in Germany. At the age of fifteen, she married a nobleman, with whom she enjoyed a happy marriage. Inspired by the example of St. Elizabeth of Hungary, a Thuringian princess who had renounced her royal station to embrace poverty as a Franciscan tertiary, Jutta attempted to conform her life, and that of her family, to the principles of the Gospel: charity, service, and a spirit of poverty.

While on pilgrimage to the Holy Land, Jutta's husband died, leaving her to raise their children alone. When, over time, each one of them entered religious life, she was free to pursue her heart's desire. After giving away all her property to the poor, she donned a simple dress and became a wandering pilgrim. Though many were moved by her piety and the austerity she had exchanged for her previous privilege, others greeted her conduct with derision.

Jutta liked to say there were three things that brought one nearer to God: painful illness, exile from home, and voluntary poverty. She experienced all three. Eventually she made her way to a distant corner of Prussia, where she became a Third Order Franciscan and took up residence as a solitary hermit. Many visitors found a path to her home, whether seeking nursing care, consolation in their troubles, or spiritual counsel.

She died at the age of sixty and was later embraced as a patroness of Prussia.

All my treasures are yours, and yours are mine.

— MESSAGE OF CHRIST, AS RECEIVED BY ST. JUTTA

ॐ ⬧ ॐ

BLESSED GILES OF ASSISI
Early Franciscan Friar
(CA. 1190–1262)
. . . .

St. Francis liked to refer to Brother Giles, one of his original followers, as "the Knight of Our Round Table." He especially commended Giles for his simplicity and his spirit of poverty. For some years Giles accompanied Francis on his preaching tours. When the saint had finished preaching, Giles would turn to the people and say, "What he says is true! Listen to him!" Believing that Lady Humility was the best preacher, he advised a brother who wished to preach in the piazza of Perugia to proclaim in his sermon: "Boo, boo; much I talk, but little I do."

Eventually, after Francis encouraged him to go forth and spread the Gospel, he went on pilgrimages to Compostela in Spain, to Rome, and to the Holy Land. Wherever he went, he insisted on working in exchange for alms. A mission to Tunis to preach to the Muslims there ended in failure when local Christians, afraid of stirring up trouble, implored him to return to his ship.

Brother Giles spent much time contemplating the joys of heaven. Just the mention of a word like *paradise* would incite him to ecstasy—a fact mischievously exploited by street urchins whenever they saw him approaching.

In *The Life of Brother Giles* by Brother Leo, it is noted that Giles possessed "seven very praiseworthy and wholesome and perfect qualities." These included his faith, reverence, devotion, compassion, consideration, and obedience. "The seventh, that he was beloved by God and men because of the graces which were showered on him."

Giles outlived most of the original friars. Yet the sad year of Francis's death in 1226 was capped for Giles by an appearance from the Lord—the greatest event of his life, he said, after his birth, his baptism, and the day he took the habit. He retired to a hermitage in Perugia where he spent most of his time in silence. He died on April 23, 1262. He was beatified in 1777.

He who does good to his own soul also does good to the souls of his friends.

—BLESSED GILES OF ASSISI

St. Isabel of France
Franciscan Princess
(1225–1270)
· · · · · · · · ·

Beautiful, clever, and the daughter of a king (Louis VIII of France), Princess Isabel was destined for a life of pomp and luxury. But her heart was drawn elsewhere. When her frequent fasts and austerity caused her to fall ill, her mother consulted a holy woman, who told her that when Isabel recovered she should be considered as dead to the world. So it was. Isabel refused all proposals of marriage—even when urged on her by Pope Innocent IV, who said that her marriage would serve the good of Christendom. She insisted on serving God before all else.

Increasingly, Isabel felt attracted to the Franciscan movement that was sweeping Europe. At dinner each day she would welcome a number of poor people, whom she waited on personally. In the evenings she would leave the palace to visit the sick. When her brother Louis ascended the throne, he agreed to support her plan to establish a Franciscan convent in Longchamps. St. Bonaventure himself helped to devise its rule. It was called the Monastery of the Humility of the Virgin Mary.

Isabel did not formally join the enclosed community. Instead, she lived in quarters separate from the nuns and continued to wear secular clothing, while devoting herself to prayer and contemplation. She died in 1270.

We beheld in her a mirror of innocence, and at the same time an admirable model of penance, a lily of purity, a fragrant rose of patience and self-renunciation, an endless fountain of goodness and mercy.

—FROM *The Life of Isabel of France*

꽃 φ 꽃

Blessed Jacoba of Settesoli
Third Order Franciscan
(1190–1273)
· · · · · · · · ·

Jacoba of Settesoli was a young widow living in Rome. From the moment she first learned about Francis of Assisi, she longed to meet him. That opportunity arose when Francis and his companions traveled to Rome to seek the pope's approval for their new order. After hearing the saint preach, Jacoba approached and asked how she might also follow in his path. Because she still had children to raise, Francis advised her not to give up her home. "A perfect life can be lived anywhere," he said. "Poverty is everywhere. Charity is everywhere."

Following this counsel, Jacoba joined the Third Order of St. Francis, turned over administration of her property to her sons, and devoted herself to prayer and charitable works. She nevertheless remained close to Francis. He gave her a pet lamb, which used to follow her about. As Francis was nearing death, he sent Jacoba a message, urging her to come quickly and to bring a shroud for his body and wax candles for his burial.

She hastened to Assisi, doing as he had asked. She also brought with her a batch of his favorite almond cookies. At first there was consternation among the brothers about allowing a woman into the friary, but Francis interceded and welcomed her as "Brother Jacoba." Thus, she was admitted and so she remained beside him until his death. Afterward he was buried in her shroud.

Jacoba remained in Assisi until her own death on February 8, 1273. She was buried near the tomb of St. Francis.

While I was praying a voice within me said, "Go, visit your father, blessed Francis, without delay, and hurry, because if you delay long you will not find him alive."

— BLESSED JACOBA OF SETTESOLI

✧ ☙ ✧

St. Bonaventure

Minister General of the Order, Doctor of the Church

(1221–1274)

· · · · · · · · ·

Bonaventure, who was born to a wealthy family in Orvieto, joined the Franciscans around 1238 in the midst of his studies at the University of Paris. St. Francis had died only some dozen years before, but already his order was rapidly changing the face of the Church in Europe. To Bonaventure, it seemed that the Franciscan Order "was not invented by human providence but by Christ. In it, the learned and the simple lived as brethren."

Bonaventure himself was definitely one of the learned. Franciscan simplicity might not have seemed an attractive fit for such a scholar. In fact, Francis had held learning in great esteem so long as it was subordinated to the pursuit of holiness. In this spirit, Bonaventure received support from the Order to continue his studies. In 1257, along with his Dominican counterpart, St. Thomas Aquinas, he received his doctorate in theology.

Rather than pursue the life of an academic theologian, however, Bonaventure was immediately elected to serve as minister-general of the Friars Minor—a role in which he left a lasting mark. During a time of contending factions within the order, Bonaventure tried deftly to steer a middle course between the radical freedom of Francis and the disciplined order of a religious community. To reinforce his moderate interpretation of the Franciscan charism, he composed an influential life of St. Francis. For his successful efforts, he would become known as the Second Founder.

He wrote a number of other important works, including his mystical treatise *The Journey of the Mind to God*. This was his attempt to translate Francis's identification with Christ into philosophical terms—a journey of the soul along the path of holiness, leading from contemplation of the created world to an ever-deepening contemplation of the spiritual order, and progressing ultimately toward the goal of union with God.

In 1265, Bonaventure respectfully declined an appointment as archbishop of York. In 1273, however, Pope Gregory X ordered him to accept the title of cardinal-bishop of Albano. When papal legates arrived to present him with his red hat and insignia of office, he kept them waiting while he finished washing the dishes. Summarizing his spirituality, he observed: "The perfection of a religious man is to do common things in a perfect manner, and a constant fidelity in small matters is great and heroic virtue!"

Bonaventure died in 1274. He was canonized in 1482 and later declared a Doctor of the Church. In recognition of his angelic virtue, he is known as the Seraphic Doctor.

༺✠༻

If you learn everything except Christ, you learn nothing. If you learn nothing except Christ, you learn everything.

—St. Bonaventure

ᘓᘎᘐ

ST. ZITA
Domestic Worker, Third Order Franciscan
(C. 1218–1278)
· · · · · · · · · · ·

St. Zita is the patron of servants and domestic workers. Such was her own station for forty-seven years of service — from the age of twelve until her death — to a wealthy family in Lucca, Italy. Early on, Zita, a member of the Third Order of St. Francis, was recognized for her unusual piety — a cause for derision among many of the household staff. She rose in the night for prayer and always attended the first Mass of the morning. But apart from such devotions, Zita considered her work itself to be an expression of her spiritual life: "A servant is not good if she is not industrious; work-shy piety in people of our position is sham piety." Gradually her qualities won respect and admiration. Her employer even overlooked her generosity to the poor. In her later years, she devoted increasing time to visiting the sick and those in prison. She had a special devotion to those under sentence of death; for these, she prayed without ceasing.

Zita died on April 27, 1278, at the age of sixty. She was canonized in 1696. Among other things, she is often invoked for help in finding lost keys.

❦

Notwithstanding her extreme attention to her exterior employments, she acquired a wonderful facility of joining with them almost continual mental prayer and of keeping her soul constantly attentive to the divine presence. Who would not imagine that such a person should have been esteemed and beloved by all who knew her?

— Butler's Lives of the Saints

ᘓᗏᗅ ⚘ ᘓᗏᗅ

St. Agnes of Bohemia
Princess and Abbess
(ca. 1203–1280)
· · · · · · · · · · · ·

Agnes was born in Prague, where her father was the king of Bohemia. Despite the privileges of her station, she enjoyed no freedom to decide her own destiny. She was simply a commodity to be invested wherever she might bring the highest return for her family and its dynastic interests. Starting at the age of three, she was shipped to various kingdoms and betrothed to strangers she had never met. Through chance or providence, all these engagements came to naught. Finally, when she was to be paired with King Henry III of England, she wrote to the pope asking him to prevent the marriage on the grounds that she wished to consecrate herself to Christ. Surprisingly, Henry yielded, granting, "If she had left me for a mortal man, I should have made my vengeance felt, but I cannot take offense if she prefers the King of Heaven to me."

What inspired this bold intention? Agnes had been deeply affected by the arrival in Prague of the first Franciscan friars, followed shortly by five Poor Clare sisters. In 1236, her royal life behind her, she formally joined them. Agnes received a number of personal letters from St. Clare, a precious window on the early Franciscan movement. Clare addressed Agnes as "the half of her soul and the special shrine of her heart's deepest love." Speaking as a "mother" to "her favorite daughter," she commended Agnes for the poverty she had chosen, thus securing a place on "the path of prudent happiness." "Place your mind before the mirror of eternity!" she counseled her. "Place your soul in the brilliance of glory! Place your heart in the figure of the divine substance! And transform your whole being into the image of the Godhead itself through contemplation."

Agnes spent forty-four years as a Poor Clare and inspired many other noble women in Europe to follow her example. She died in 1280 and was canonized in 1989.

Though you, more than others, could have enjoyed the magnificence and honor and dignity of the world, and could have been married to the illustrious Caesar with splendor befitting you and his excellency, you have rejected all things and have chosen with your whole heart and soul a life of holy poverty and destitution. Thus you took a spouse of a more noble lineage.

—St. Clare to St. Agnes of Bohemia

⟨⟨⟨ ♱ ⟩⟩⟩

Blessed Benedict Sinigardi

Franciscan Friar

(1190–1282)

· · · · · · · · ·

Benedict Sinigardi was born to a wealthy and noble family in Arezzo. In 1211, he heard St. Francis preach in his town, and his heart was immediately won. Abandoning his life of luxury, he was welcomed into the Order of Friars Minor, receiving his habit from St. Francis himself. At twenty-seven, he was appointed provincial of the Marche region. Afterward, he was sent on a missionary journey that took him to Greece, Romania, and Turkey. He built the first Franciscan monastery in Constantinople and then went on to the Holy Land, where he served as provincial for sixteen years. In his old age, he returned to Arezzo, where he died in 1282.

There are no surviving writings by Blessed Benedict, but he is credited with establishing the Angelus Prayer, a commemoration of the Incarnation, which became one of the most popular devotions in Christendom. Deriving its name from the first words, "The Angel of the Lord declared unto Mary," the prayer consists of the recital of three verses from Scripture with an accompanying response, interspersed by a Hail Mary. It was traditionally recited three times a day, and in many towns in Europe it is still signaled by the ringing of church bells at noon.

CRACP CRA

It is very suggestive that we stop in the middle of the day for a moment of Marian prayer. It is now unique, because we are in the place where, according to tradition, it was the custom to recite the Angelus Domini.

—POPE JOHN PAUL II, IN A VISIT TO AREZZO IN 1993

ᝦ☞ ⌗ ᜒᝦ

St. Kunigunde of Poland
Queen and Abbess
(c. 1224–1292)
· · · · · · · · · · ·

St. Kunigunde (or Kinga) was the daughter of the king of Hungary and a niece of St. Elizabeth of Hungary. At the age of sixteen, she was married to King Boleslaus V of Poland. She waited until the night of their wedding, according to legend, to reveal that she had vowed herself to God and to a life of celibacy. Fortunately, her husband agreed to honor her wishes, thus earning the title Boleslaus the Chaste.

It was a happy marriage for the next forty years. Kunigunde wore a hair shirt and practiced other forms of mortification. From her personal fortune she endowed many churches, hospitals, and monasteries, and when her husband died, she retired from court and became a Poor Clare in a convent she had established. There she refused any acknowledgment of her former status, and devoted herself to prayer. In time, she became prioress. During an invasion of Tartars, the nuns were forced to flee. When the castle in which they found refuge was besieged, Kunigunde's prayers were credited with the invaders' withdrawal. She died on July 24, 1292. In 1999, she was canonized by Pope John Paul II.

A famous Polish legend credits St. Kunigunde with the discovery of a great salt mine in Poland. An underground chapel built in this mine, "St. Kinga's Chapel," is listed by UNESCO as a World Heritage site.

⤫

Saints do not fade away. What is the name of that power which defies the inexorable law that says, "Everything fades away?" The name of this power is love.

—Pope John Paul II on the canonization of St. Kunigunde

St. Margaret of Cortona

Third Order Franciscan

(1247–1297)
· · · · · · · · · ·

St. Margaret was raised in a poor family in Tuscany. Following the death of her mother when Margaret was just eleven, a new stepmother turned her out of the house. Eventually, with few apparent options, she eloped with a young nobleman, who kept her as his mistress. Though she bore him a son, he would not marry her. When he was eventually murdered, Margaret took this as a sign of God's judgment on her life. Penniless, she returned to her father's house, but he would not take her in. Now homeless as well as destitute, she made her way to Cortona, where she had heard of the compassion of the Franciscan friars. She introduced herself by walking through town with a rope around her neck, a sign of her penitence. The friars quickly urged her to quit this spectacle and also curbed her proclivity for extremes of asceticism. Eventually she was accepted as a Franciscan tertiary. With other women she formed a nursing community, caring for the sick and the poor. Nevertheless, stories of her former life continued to generate gossip. She observed, "I see more Pharisees among Christians than surrounded Pilate."

Over time, as reports spread of her holiness and her purported miracles, as well as her private colloquies with Christ, Margaret attracted more positive attention. The Franciscans urged her to embark on a public crusade to call sinners to conversion. Penitents from all over Italy, and as far away as France and Spain, made their way to Cortona to hear her spiritual discourses.

She died on February 22, 1297. She was canonized in 1728.

Show now that thou art converted; call others to repentance…. The graces I have bestowed on thee are not meant for thee alone.

—A MESSAGE FROM THE LORD TO
ST. MARGARET OF CORTONA

ﾟ⌘ﾟ

St. Louis of Anjou
Franciscan Bishop
(1274–1297)
· · · · · · · · · ·

Louis was born to a royal family. His father, Charles II, was king of Naples and Sicily. This had its downside. When Charles was taken prisoner in a battle with the king of Aragon, he agreed to secure his release by surrendering his three sons as hostages. Thus, Louis remained a prisoner in Barcelona for seven years. Yet he did not find this arrangement uncongenial. Impressed by the Franciscan friars who tutored him, he vowed one day to join them.

Upon Louis's release in 1295, his father tried to arrange his marriage to the daughter of his former captor. Louis refused. What is more, he insisted on surrendering his title. "Jesus Christ is my kingdom," he said. "If he is all I have, I shall have everything. If I don't have him, I lose everything." Though his family acceded to his wish, they drew the line at his becoming a Franciscan.

When Louis was twenty-three, a further setback to his desire for a simple life came when Pope Boniface VIII appointed him bishop of Toulouse. There was, of course, the matter of his first being ordained a priest. Louis agreed on condition that he could make a religious profession among the Friars Minor, thereby fulfilling his childhood dream. Clothed in a tattered habit, he appeared on foot in his new bishopric. Stripping the episcopal palace of all luxury, he set an example of simplicity for the whole diocese. But he hated the burden of office, and after only three months he asked to resign. Permission was denied. Nevertheless, he soon fell ill and died a few months later, on August 19, 1297.

Louis was canonized in 1317. The famous mission of San Luis Obispo in California was named for him.

⬥

After a dangerous voyage, at last I am in sight of the port I have been trying to get to for so long. I shall now be able to enjoy my God…and I shall be freed from a heavy load which I just can't bear.

—ST. LOUIS OF ANJOU, ON HIS DEATHBED

Blessed Jacopone of Todi
Franciscan Poet
(1230–1306)
· · · · · · · · ·

Jacopone Benedetti was a prosperous lawyer in the Umbrian town of Todi. His life took a tragic turn one day when his young wife was killed in an accident. This terrible loss was compounded by the belated discovery of his wife's piety. As she lay dying before his eyes, he loosened her gown and was surprised and deeply moved to find that she wore a secret hair shirt, a penance he believed she must have undertaken to atone for his own sins.

His world in ruins and his ambitions laid bare, Jacopone quit his profession, gave away all his belongings, and became a public penitent—to all appearances, a kind of wandering fool. For ten years he maintained this life of aimless poverty and penance. Then, at the age of forty-eight, he knocked on the door of the Franciscans and applied for admission.

Remarkably, in joining the Franciscans he also found a new voice as a poet—indeed, one of the great lyric poets of the Middle Ages. In the passionate language of love, his mystical poems described the soul's yearning for Christ. But they retained a mournful undertone, the accent of a faith born in loss. Among his most famous poems is the *Stabat Mater Dolorosa*, a heart-breaking meditation on the sorrows of Mary at the foot of the cross.

At the cross her station keeping,

Stood the mournful Mother weeping,

Close to Jesus to the last:

Through her heart, His sorrow sharing,

All His bitter anguish bearing,

Now at length the sword had passed.

Jacopone was a leader of the Spirituals, a Franciscan party dedicated to the most radical form of apostolic poverty. The Spirituals ran into conflict with the worldly Pope Boniface VIII, whose legitimacy they challenged. After addressing a bitter manifesto to the pope, Jacopone was imprisoned for five years. Only after Boniface's death was he freed to live out the rest of his life as a hermit. He died on Christmas Day in 1306.

Here lie the bones of Jacopone of Todi, Friar Minor, who, having gone mad with love of Christ, by a new artifice deceived the world and took heaven by violence.

—Inscription on the tomb of
Blessed Jacopone of Todi

BLESSED JOHN DUNS SCOTUS
Franciscan Theologian
(CA. 1266–1308)
· · · · · · · · · · · ·

John Duns, later known as the Subtle Doctor, was called Scotus on account of his birth in Scotland. He entered the Franciscans at the age of fifteen and was later ordained a priest. After studies in Oxford and Paris, he went on to hold teaching positions in Paris and Cologne, where he was acclaimed as one of the greatest of the Scholastic theologians. His mystically charged theology held particular charm for the Franciscans, rendering in philosophical terms the creation-centered spirituality of their holy founder.

Like other scholastic theologians, Duns Scotus tried to present a philosophical "proof" for the existence of God. In his case, he focused on the observation that all things require some prior cause for their existence. From this, he predicated the existence of a primary infinite cause which owes its existence to itself alone. Yet he drew a distinction between what could be "proved" by reason and what could be known only by faith. There was a difference between a rational knowledge of the existence of God and a saving knowledge of the *love* of God.

Duns Scotus defined God as infinite love. He taught that the incarnation was not required as payment for sin; it was willed through eternity as an expression of God's love, and hence God's desire for consummated union with creation. Our redemption by the cross was likewise an expression of God's love and compassion rather than an appeasement of God's anger or a form of compensation for God's injured majesty. He believed that knowledge of God's love should evoke a loving response on the part of humanity. He wrote, "I am of the opinion that God wished to redeem us in this fashion principally in order to draw us to his love." Through our own loving self-gift, he argued, we join with Christ in becoming "co-lovers" of the Holy Trinity.

Unlike philosophers in the line of Plato, Scotus did not value the ideal at the expense of the real. Created things pointed to their Creator not only by their conformity to an ideal pattern but by their individuality and uniqueness—what he termed their "thisness" (*haecceitas*). Thus, the path to contemplation should proceed not only through the mind but through the senses. This insight of Scotus especially endeared him to the most highly distinctive of Catholic poets, the Jesuit Gerard Manley Hopkins. He paid tribute to the Subtle Doctor in one of his poems:

> Of realty the rarest-veined unraveller; a not
> Rivalled insight, be rival Italy or Greece.

Duns Scotus died on November 8, 1308. He was beatified in 1993.

O Lord, our God.... Teach your servant to show by reason what he holds with faith most certain, that you are the most eminent, the first efficient cause and the last end.

—BLESSED JOHN DUNS SCOTUS

༄ ༁ ༂

St. Angela of Foligno
Mystic, Third Order Franciscan
(1248–1309)

. . . .

St. Angela came from a wealthy family in Foligno, Italy, where her early life was given over to frivolity and pleasure seeking. She married a rich man and bore three sons. But her existence lacked a higher purpose. By the time she was thirty-seven, she found her life such a burden that she desperately prayed to St. Francis for some relief. The next day, while sitting in church, she vowed to transform her life.

The opportunity for radical change came through tragic circumstances: the death of her entire family during an outbreak of plague. Yet, in her loss, Angela discerned the hand of God leading her to a life of penance and prayer. While standing before a crucifix she was moved, in a gesture reminiscent of Francis, to strip off all her fine clothing and to offer her life to Christ's service. During a subsequent pilgrimage to Assisi she was overwhelmed by the love of God. After giving away all her property, she joined the Third Order of St. Francis and resolved to live on alms.

In time, Angela gathered around herself a family of Franciscan tertiaries, both men and women, for whom she served as spiritual mother. In her extensive writings, she described her intimacy with God and her vivid contemplation of Christ's passion.

Her intense mystical experiences, however, did not distract her from concern for others. With her companions she nursed the sick and waited on the poor. "The world," she said, "is great with God."

One Holy Thursday she exhorted her companions, "Let us go and look for Christ our Lord. We will go to the hospital and perhaps among the sick and suffering we shall find Him." She had them beg for food, which they brought to the hospital: "And so we offered food to these poor sick people and then we washed the feet of the women and the men's hands, as they lay lonely and forsaken on their wretched pallets…." Thus, she concluded, they had successfully fulfilled their quest to find Christ on that Holy Thursday.

Angela died on January 4, 1309. She was canonized by Pope Francis in 2013.

❧ ☩ ☙

In an excess of wonder I cried out: "This world is pregnant with God!" Wherefore I understood how small is the whole of creation…but the power of God fills it all to overflowing.

—St. Angela of Foligno

❧✧❧

Blessed Ramón Lull
Missionary and Martyr, Third Order Franciscan
(1232–1316)
· · · · · · · · ·

Ramón Lull was born in Majorca in 1232, the son of a Catalan military chief. His early life was spent in the frivolity of court life. At the age of thirty, however, prompted by a recurrent vision of Jesus on the cross, he underwent a dramatic and total conversion. Afterward, he gave up all his property to his family and the poor and determined to devote his life to God's cause. In particular, he felt called to bring the Gospel to the Muslims—a vocation, he was sure, that would cost him his life.

He prepared for this mission with zeal. For over a decade he pursued studies in Latin and Arabic and immersed himself—to a remarkable degree—in the literature of Muslim religion and philosophy. He believed that a missionary must be fully knowledgeable about the beliefs of those he wished to convert.

At this point, the primary locus of Christian-Muslim encounter had been the battlefields of the Crusades. To most Christians of Lull's day, the Muslims were irredeemable heretics whose slaughter brought glory to God. The Crusades were not even ostensibly concerned with the conversion of Muslims; their object was simply to drive the "infidels" from the Holy Land, a sacred cause that justified any means. (A bright exception was St. Francis of Assisi.)

At sixty, Lull himself became a Franciscan tertiary. His vision never advanced so far as to reject all recourse to force in the service of the Gospel. But in his respect for the intelligence and good faith of non-Christians and his belief in the need to encounter them on their own terms he introduced a remarkably progressive path for this time.

Lull traveled throughout Europe lobbying and seeking sponsors for his projects, which included a series of missionary colleges where the best preachers of the world could study the languages and cultures of the non-Christian world. Such plans came to naught. He also wrote several hundred major works, as well as mystical poetry and allegorical romances about the Christian life. A Christian troubadour in the Franciscan mold, he has been called "the Catalan Dante."

Lull made three trips to North Africa. On the first and second occasions, he was quickly arrested and deported. However, on his third trip in Tunisia he was accosted by a mob on June 29, 1316, and stoned to death. He had foreseen this fate from the outset of his vocation. As he wrote, "Missionaries will convert the world by preaching, but also through the shedding of tears and blood and with great labor, and through a bitter death."

He was beatified in 1847.

But Jesus Christ, of His great clemency,
Five times upon the Cross appear'd to me,
That I might think upon Him lovingly,
And cause His Name proclaim'd abroad to be
Through all the world.

—Blessed Ramón Lull

DANTE ALIGHIERI

Poet

(1265–1321)

· · · · · · · · · ·

Dante Alighieri, one of the great literary geniuses of all time, was also a man of action, committed to social justice and the affairs of his native Florence. But he was at the same time a man of deep faith, a visionary and a prophet, who judged the world and the Church by the light of the Gospel and the radiance of eternity. All these factors combined in *The Divine Comedy* to create an artistic, as well as spiritual, masterpiece.

Florence in Dante's time was bitterly divided between rival factions, one favoring the temporal power of the pope and the other committed to the autonomy of the city. Influenced by the radical Spiritual Franciscans, Dante opposed the papal claims to temporal power—particularly the worldly statecraft of the reigning pontiff, Boniface VIII—and urged a return to the evangelical ideals of poverty and simplicity. When the political tide turned against him, he was forced to flee Florence. His enemies invented charges of corruption and he was sentenced, in absentia, to be burned at the stake should he ever return. As a result, he spent the last twenty years of his life in exile. As he later wrote, "I have been truly a ship without sail or rudder, carried to many ports and straits and shores by the dry wind blown by grievous poverty."

In these years, Dante wrote his *Divine Comedy*, the record of an imaginative pilgrimage from the depths of hell, up the mount of purgatory, and finally to the ethereal rapture of paradise. The poet's journey involves his own progressive conversion, preparing him to endure the increasingly rarefied atmosphere along his spiritual path until he is drawn into the presence of "the Love that moves the Sun and the other stars."

There is conflicting evidence about whether Dante himself was a member of the Third Order of St. Francis. There is no doubt that his spiritual vision was deeply shaped by the Franciscan movement. St. Francis himself makes a significant appearance in *Paradiso*, the third volume of the *Comedy*, where he models the poverty and humility that Dante, the pilgrim, must learn to adopt. (Dante also contrasts the saintliness of Francis with the corruption and compromises that, he believed, had overtaken his order.)

Dante died in Ravenna in 1321, far from the city he loved. He was buried in the Franciscan church.

⧉✢⧉

What then I saw is more than tongue can say.
Our human speech is dark before the vision.
The ravished memory swoons and falls away.
I saw within its depth how It conceives
all things in a single volume bound by Love,
of which the universe is the scattered leaves.

—DANTE

☙ ✠ ❧

BLESSED ODORIC OF PORDENONE
Franciscan Missionary
(CA. 1285–1331)
· · · · · · · · · · ·

Odoric of Pordenone passed his early life unremarkably as a Franciscan friar, a vocation he had embraced at the age of fifteen. In 1317, however, some impulse inspired him to embark on a fantastic journey that took him to the ends of the known world and back again.

Starting in Venice he sailed east, traveling overland from Constantinople to Baghdad and the Persian Gulf. From there he sailed to Malabar and southern India where he spent time with the ancient Christian community there. Still, he pushed on, to Ceylon, Sumatra, and Java, then north to Canton and the great ports of China. He spent several years in Beijing before turning homeward through Tibet and the capital of Lhasa, on to Persia, and eventually back to Italy.

The reasons for his travel are mysterious. As for his decision to spend his final years in seclusion, he is said to have complied with a vision from St. Francis, who ordered him to stay put. He did dictate an account of his journeys, which circulated widely. While providing little information about his activities or the motive for his grand tour, his travelogue offered an eyewitness account of the extraordinary things he had witnessed, including the curious customs, the prodigious sights, and the religious practices of the people he encountered.

Odoric died on January 14, 1331. He was beatified in 1755.

As I, friar Odoric, have travelled among the remote nations of the unbelievers, where I saw and heard many great and wonderful things, I have thought fit to relate all these things truly.

—Blessed Odoric of Pordenone

ॐ☥ॐ

St. Elizabeth of Portugal

Queen, Third Order Franciscan

(1271–1336)
· · · · · · · · ·

St. Elizabeth of Portugal was the daughter of the king of Aragon. At twelve, she married King Denis of Portugal, a profligate man, who tolerated his wife's piety while making no secret of his own infidelities. Elizabeth bore him two children, a son and a daughter. Her son, Alfonso, would later come close to open rebellion against his neglectful father. For her role in effecting a reconciliation between father and son, Elizabeth became popularly known as "the Peacemaker." But her peace-making talents were exercised on an even greater level when she personally prevented a war between Portugal and Castile.

Elizabeth lived up to her public responsibilities as queen. But the greater part of her time was spent in prayer and a variety of charitable projects. She established hospitals, orphanages, and religious houses throughout the kingdom, as well as halfway homes for "fallen women." "God made me queen so that I may serve others," she noted.

When her husband died, she put on the habit of a Franciscan tertiary and lived for her eleven remaining years in one of the monasteries she had helped to found. She emerged occasionally to intercede between rival monarchs—with most of whom she bore some relation. Even as she lived she was credited with miracles, and she was revered by the people of Portugal.

Elizabeth died in 1336 and was canonized three centuries later by Pope Urban VIII, who named her the Patroness of Peace.

⌘

> Do not forget that when sovereigns are at war they can no longer busy themselves with their administration; justice is not distributed; no care is taken of the people, and this alone is your sovereign charge, this the main point of your duty as kings.
>
> —St. Elizabeth of Portugal

St. Conrad of Piacenza

Third Order Franciscan

(CA. 1290–1351)

· · · · · · · · · · · ·

St. Conrad, a young nobleman from Piacenza, was out hunting one day when, in order to drive out his game, he ordered his servants to set fire to the surrounding brushwood. Following a sudden turn in the wind, Conrad watched in horror as the fire consumed the neighboring fields. After returning quietly to town, he said nothing about his part in this disaster. But when a peasant was subsequently charged with the crime and sentenced to death, Conrad was filled with remorse. Stepping forward, he accepted the blame and paid for all the damages, though this left him nearly ruined. In this misfortune, however, Conrad saw the hand of God. Subsequently, he and his wife decided to give up all their property and pursue religious life. While his wife entered a convent of Poor Clares, Conrad entered the Third Order of St. Francis, joining a group of hermits in the Valley of Noto.

Contrary to his intentions, Conrad's sacrifice caused him to be widely admired. To escape the throng of visitors, he retired to a remote grotto. But when his prayers were credited with ending a famine, he felt he had no choice but to welcome the stream of suffering pilgrims who came seeking his intervention. Many other miracles were credited to Conrad, and birds were reported to flutter over his head whenever he exited his hermitage. Discerning that his final hour had arrived, he lay on the ground in front of a crucifix and died on February 19, 1351. He was canonized in 1625.

If the sinner do penance for his sins, and do judgment and justice, and restore the pledge and render what he has robbed, he shall surely live and shall not die.

—Ezekiel 33:14–15

ᏫᏫᏪᏫᏪ

BLESSED MICHELINA OF PESARO
Widow and Third Order Franciscan
(1300–1356)
· · · · · · · · · ·

Blessed Michelina was born in the town of Pesaro, on the east coast of Italy. At twelve she married a wealthy member of the powerful Malatesta family and went on to enjoy a rich and frivolous social life. By twenty, however, she found herself a widow with a young son. He became the center of her life. A Franciscan tertiary named Syriaca, whom she had befriended, urged her to put aside worldly occupations and devote herself to God, but Michelina resisted this counsel. When her son subsequently fell ill and died, however, she put on the habit of a Franciscan tertiary, gave away her possessions to the poor, and took to begging alms from door to door.

Her sudden embrace of voluntary poverty did not inspire a corresponding charity on the part of her neighbors. Her family, thinking her mad, had her confined. In time, however, they were won over by her evident sincerity, and she was free to dedicate herself to works of mercy, especially care for the sick. In imitation of St. Francis, she had a special dedication to lepers, and there were stories of her effecting cures by the power of her kiss. Toward the end of her life, she went on pilgrimage to Rome, where she received a mystical share in the sufferings of Christ. She died on June 19, 1356. She was beatified in 1737.

༺༶༺

My God, so that I may be certain to find my son close to you, I will then renounce all the vanity of the world!

—BLESSED MICHELINA OF PESARO

❧ ✟ ❧

ST. BIRGITTA OF SWEDEN

Mystic and Prophet, Third Order Franciscan

(1303–1373)

· · · · · · · · ·

St. Birgitta of Sweden was one of the great women of the fourteenth century: the wife of a nobleman and the mother of eight children; a nun and founder of monasteries as well as a religious order; a pilgrim who crossed continents and seas; a mystic who filled many volumes with accounts of her visions and colloquies with Christ; and a prophet who called kings to justice and popes to live up to their sacred duties.

She experienced her first vision as a child, when she saw an altar, and seated above it a woman who said, "Come, Birgitta," and offered her a crown. Some years later she had another vision of Christ hanging on the cross. When she asked him who had treated him this way, he answered, "They who despise me and spurn my love for them." From that point, she felt herself mystically united with Christ and determined to serve him in every way.

At fourteen, she married a prince named Ulf. It was a happy marriage that lasted twenty-eight years. Whenever she could, she would visit the hospitals, binding the wounds of the patients with her own hands. She often brought along her young children, desiring that they learn "at an early age to serve God and his poor and sick." Eventually, fed up with the frivolity of court life, both she and Ulf embarked on a long pilgrimage that took them all the way to Compostela in Spain. On the return trip, Ulf died, and Birgitta sought consolation in becoming a member of the Third Order of St. Francis.

Before long, she received another vision, this time instructing her to found a monastery in Sweden. After she had accomplished this, she went on yet another pilgrimage to the Holy Land, where she again received many visions of the events of Christ's life, before finally settling in Rome for the last twenty years of her life. Wherever she traveled, she spoke out against slavery, injustice, and threats to peace. Confronting the corruption she encountered in the Eternal City, she cried out, "O Rome, Rome, be converted and turn to the Lord thy God." She excoriated the pope for abandoning Rome for Avignon, and at one point even denounced him as "a murderer of souls, worse than Lucifer, more unjust than Pilate, more merciless than Judas." Despite her frankness, he approved the rule of her new order, the Brigittines.

St. Birgitta died on July 23, 1373. A triumphal procession, led by her daughter, accompanied her body across Europe and back to her abbey in Vadstena, where she was laid to rest.

The people of earth have need of a triple mercy: sorrow for their sins, penance to atone for them, and strength to do good.

— St. Birgitta of Sweden

☙ ⚜ ❧

St. Roch

Penitent, Third Order Franciscan

(CA. 1348–CA. 1378)

. . . .

The Third Order of St. Francis has traditionally claimed St. Roch as a member, and his name appears on the calendar of Franciscan saints. But little is known of his actual life. According to legend, he was born to a noble family in Montpellier, France. At the age of twenty, when his parents died, he renounced his fortune and took up the life of a mendicant pilgrim. While on a journey to Rome, he encountered a number of plague-stricken cities. There he courageously nursed the sick and effected many cures, supposedly by making the sign of the cross.

Eventually, Roch himself was struck by the plague. Rather than seek help in a hospital, he dragged himself into the woods to die. There he was discovered by a dog who brought him food and cured him by licking his wounds. Upon recovering, he resumed his ministry, caring for the sick and curing many people, along with their livestock. Eventually he returned to Montpellier, where he died.

For many centuries St. Roch was invoked as a protector against plague and pestilence. He is often depicted in the company of a dog—whose memory, some have argued, deserves equal veneration.

O Jesu, my Saviour, I thank thee that thou puttest me to affliction like to thine other servants, by this odious ardour of pestilence, and most meek Lord, I beseech thee to this desert place, give the comfort of thy grace.

—St. Roch

༅༔འ༔ཕ༔འ༔

BLESSED JOAN MARY DE MAILLE
Third Order Franciscan
(1332–1414)
· · · · · · · · · ·

Blessed Joan was born to a noble family in France. As a child, it was said that her prayers had saved a neighbor boy, Robert de Sillé, after he fell into a pond and nearly drowned. When Joan turned sixteen, she and Robert were married. Although they elected to maintain a celibate relationship, they were apparently a devoted couple and together they adopted and raised three orphans. During an invasion by the English, Robert was taken captive and held for ransom. He managed to escape, and afterward he and Joan devoted themselves to the ransom of other prisoners.

This charity infuriated Robert's family. Upon Robert's death in 1362, they expelled Joan from their house. For several years she supported herself as best she could, eventually learning to prepare medicines and becoming a Franciscan tertiary. But for a while she was reduced to living in pigsties and dog kennels. When her in-laws eventually restored her property, she gave it all to the Carthusians, and at the age of fifty-seven retired to a small room in Tours, where she devoted herself to prayer and works of mercy. Though some considered her mad, many others recognized her evident holiness. She was known for her gift of prophecy and her special dedication to prisoners—whether criminals or captives of war. At one time, she even persuaded the king to release all the prisoners of Tours. She died on March 28, 1414, and was beatified in 1871.

༺༝༻

I was a prisoner, and you visited me.

—MATTHEW 25:36

⚜ ✿ ⚜

BLESSED ANGELINA OF MARSCIANO

Founder, Franciscan Sisters of the Third Order Regular

(CA. 1377–1435)

· · · · · · · · · · · ·

Angelina, who was raised in a noble family, married the count of Civitella when she was fifteen. Two years later, her husband died, and Angelina inherited his title and castle. Straightaway, she put on the habit of a Franciscan tertiary and gathered her female attendants into a religious community. Together they began to travel throughout the region, calling sinners to conversion and extolling the virtues of virginity. So effective were her paeans to virginity that she was deemed a threat to civil order. Placed under arrest, she was denounced as a witch (because of her sway over young girls) and a heretic (because of her supposed rejection of marriage). Yet, when she was brought before King Ladislas of Naples, who was fully prepared to have her burned, she mounted an effective defense. "If I have taught or practiced error," she sad, "I am prepared to suffer the appropriate punishment." With that she drew back her cloak to reveal burning embers, hidden within. The king was sufficiently impressed that he spared her the worst punishment. Still, he exiled her from the kingdom.

On pilgrimage to Assisi, Angelina received a vision that she should found an enclosed monastery of the Third Order Regular of St. Francis in Foligno. In 1397, with support from the local bishop, she accomplished this plan. Other communities gradually affiliated with her convent, and they were recognized as a new congregation in 1428. Angelina died on July 14, 1435. She was beatified in 1825.

❦

Behold the fire!

—Blessed Angelina of Marsciano

St. Colette
Reformer of the Poor Clares
(1381–1447)
· · · · · · · · · ·

St. Colette was born to a poor family in Picardy, France. Upon the death of her parents, she was cared for by the local abbey where her father had worked. Naturally drawn to contemplative life, she became a Third Order Franciscan and afterward received permission to enter an enclosed cell attached to the church. There she spent four years in solitude and prayer, until one day, on the feast of St. Francis, she received an extraordinary vision. She saw Francis and the Blessed Mother begging Christ to put her in charge of reforming the Franciscan Order. In an audience with Peter de Luna—recognized by the French, in this time of papal schism, as Pope Benedict XIII— he endorsed her mission and appointed her superior of any convent she might found or reform.

At once, this uneducated young maid of twenty-four set off on a tour of all the Poor Clare houses in France. She met with wide scorn and even violent opposition. In more than one case, she was accused of sorcery. Yet the tide began to turn. In all, she founded seventeen new convents and restored to many others the strict poverty of the primitive rule of St. Clare. Her reform also spread to a number of friaries, and many noble families sought her wisdom and counsel. She was sustained by a deep discipline of prayer, and every Friday she received a vision of Jesus on the cross. Like her master, St. Francis, she was drawn to animals, especially lambs and birds, which she easily tamed.

She died in 1447 and was canonized in 1807.

Blessed be the hour in which our Lord Jesus Christ, God and Man was born. Blessed be the Holy Spirit by whom he was conceived. Blessed be the glorious Virgin Mary of whom the Incarnate Word was born.

—St. Colette

∽✿∽

St. Catherine of Bologna
Abbess, Poor Clare
(1413–1463)
· · · · · · · · ·

St. Catherine was raised in luxury in a noble family in Bologna. Yet, at fourteen, she persuaded her family to let her join a community of Franciscan tertiaries. From an early age she had experienced visions of Jesus, "who would enter into her soul like a radiant sunshine to establish there the profoundest peace." But there were also demonic thoughts that sometimes plunged her into despair. Through constant prayer she vanquished such doubts, and one night during the Christmas Vigil she was rewarded by a vision of the Blessed Mother, who offered her the great privilege of holding her infant Son. "I leave you to picture the joy of this poor creature," she wrote, "when she found herself holding the Son of the eternal Father in her arms. Trembling with respect, but still more overcome with joy, she took the liberty of caressing Him, of pressing Him against her heart and of bringing His face to her lips…"

After some years Catherine was directed to take charge of a convent of Poor Clares in Bologna. Her reputed gifts of healing and prophecy—as well as her deep kindness—attracted many novices. Whenever she had to correct a young sister, she would insist on sharing in her punishment. When one of the novices was tempted to leave, Catherine pledged to take her place in purgatory until the end of time if only she would remain. (The novice stayed.)

Among her last instructions: "If you would have all, you must give all." She died on March 9, 1463, and was canonized in 1712. Apart from several devotional books, Catherine left behind a number of hymns and paintings. She is honored as a patron of artists.

It means little to wear a worn habit and walk with bowed head; to be truly humble one has to know how to bear humiliation. It is the touchstone of Christian discipleship.

—St. Catherine of Bologna

⌘

BLESSED MARK OF MONTEGALLO

Franciscan Friar

(1425–1496)

· · · · · · · · ·

Blessed Mark, who was born in Montegallo, Italy, studied medicine, married, and worked as a doctor for some years. At a certain point, he and his wife both agreed that their true vocations were to religious life. So they parted, she to become a Poor Clare, while he entered the Franciscan community in Fabriano. After his talents as a preacher were discovered, he embarked on a preaching tour that essentially lasted forty years. In prayer one day he heard a voice that said, "Brother Mark, preach love!" This became his central theme—the love of God and one's neighbor.

In his dedication to the poor, Mark sought to find a remedy for the terrible suffering caused by predatory loan sharks. He established what were called *monti di pieta*—essentially pawn shops that offered small loans in exchange for some modest collateral. Later these became banks that lent money at little or no interest. He easily raised the necessary funds through his preaching.

Eventually, age and the strenuousness of his itinerant ministry caught up with him. In Vicenza, where he lay dying on March 19, 1496, he asked to hear the Passion read aloud. Upon hearing the words, "It is consummated," he breathed his last.

❧ ✠ ☙

A new star of love.

—A name applied to Blessed Mark of Montegallo
after his death

BLESSED LOUISA OF SAVOY
Widow and Poor Clare
(1461–1503)
· · · · · · · · · ·

Louisa was born into the highest circle of nobility. Her father was the duke of Savoy, while on her mother's side her uncle was the king of France. A pious child, she dreamed of entering religious life. But this was hardly an acceptable vocation for a child of her station. Instead, when she was seventeen, her uncle arranged her marriage to a young nobleman. Though they would have no children, the marriage proved a happy one. Her husband accepted her religious devotion, which she combined with an active role in court life. Together they set a high moral standard, requiring that anyone who cursed in their presence make a contribution to the poor. Meanwhile, Louisa engaged in a range of charitable activities, from care for widows and orphans to nursing the sick and even victims of the plague.

When she was twenty-seven, her husband died. After a period of mourning, she made preparations to leave her privileged world—putting on the habit of a Franciscan tertiary and distributing her fortune. After two years she entered a convent of Poor Clares in Orbe. There she spent the rest of her life in prayer and poverty, eventually rising to the office of abbess. She died on July 24, 1503 and was beatified in 1839.

Farewell my beloved sisters, I am going to Paradise. It is very beautiful there!

—LAST WORDS OF BLESSED LOUISA OF SAVOY

St. Joan of Valois

Founder, Annonciades of Bourges

(1464–1505)

· · · · · · · · ·

St. Joan, daughter of King Louis XI of France, was apparently misshapen from birth, a fact that incited her father's contempt. When she was eight weeks old, he arranged her betrothal to her two-year-old cousin Louis, Duke of Orleans. The marriage transpired when Joan was twelve. Though her husband accepted the arrangement for pragmatic reasons, he felt no affection for his bride. Joan was subjected to constant abuse and ridicule in the court. She accepted all this without shame or complaint. But when Louis, after becoming king, sought to have the marriage annulled on the grounds of Joan's deformity, she resisted as best she could. In the end, however, Pope Alexander VI decided in Louis's favor, judging that the marriage had not been entered freely. Joan accepted this decision as the will of God and retired to Bourges to devote herself to a life of prayer and charity. Louis bestowed on her the title Duchess of Berry.

With the support of her Franciscan confessor, Joan established a religious foundation devoted to "the ten virtues of Our Lady." The first postulants were eleven girls from the local school—some of them not yet ten. Under a rule that eventually received papal approval, they became the Franciscan order of the Annonciades of Bourges. Publicly renouncing her title and her property, Joan embraced a life of voluntary poverty. She died within a year. Her canonization followed in 1950.

❧ ✤ ❧

If so it is to be, praised be the Lord.

—St. Joan's response to the annulment
of her marriage

St. Francis of Paola

Founder of the Minim Friars

(1416–1507)

· · · · · · · · · ·

The long-childless parents of this saint had prayed to St. Francis of Assisi for a son. When their prayers were answered, they named him Francis. No doubt their intentions exerted a powerful influence on his later vocation. At twelve, he spent a year in a Franciscan house, receiving there a basic education and acquiring a taste for asceticism. Eventually, when he was not yet fifteen, he took up the life of a hermit, living in a cave near his hometown of Paola.

In time, Francis attracted disciples, the foundation of a religious order he called the Minim Friars—a name reflecting the desire that they be counted the least in the household of God. Along with traditional religious vows, Francis added a fourth: that his followers abstain not only from meat but also from any animal products whatsoever. Beyond a spirit of penance, this strict diet also reflected the saint's determination to extend the spirit of nonviolence to all God's creatures. Among the miraculous legends associated with Francis are many involving the restoration of life to assorted animals, including a favorite trout, which a hapless cleric had caught and cooked.

In 1481, King Louis XI of France, facing death, begged Francis to come and heal him. Francis made the trip, traveling barefoot the whole way. Though he told the king that life and death were in God's hands, he managed to reconcile the king to his fate and remained by his side until the end.

Francis died on Good Friday in 1507 at the age of ninety-one.

Take pains to refrain from sharp words. Pardon one another so that later on you will not remember the injury. The recollection of an injury is itself wrong. It adds to our anger, nurtures our sins and hates what is good. It is a rusty arrow and poison for the soul. It puts all virtue to flight.

—St. Francis of Paola

St. Baptista Varano
Poor Clare
(1458–1524)

Camilla Varano was the daughter of a powerful Italian prince and his mistress. Raised by her father and his lawful wife, she was groomed for a life in the highest circles of society. For many years she embraced this world of "music, dancing, dress, and other worldly amusements." She could "not bear" the sight of monks or nuns. Then one day she heard a sermon that hit her like a thunderbolt. In response to prayer she received the gift of "three lilies": hatred of the world, a sense of unworthiness, and a willingness to suffer. Gradually she found herself attracted to religious life.

Her father did everything he could to thwart her vocation—even to the point of locking her up. But after two years, when she was twenty-three, he relented and allowed her to enter the Poor Clares, where she took the name Baptista. She likened the experience to crossing the Red Sea to escape from slavery under Pharaoh.

In the newfound freedom of the cloister, Baptista began to experience vivid mystical visions, including colloquies with St. Clare. In another case, two winged angels held her aloft to contemplate the bleeding feet of Christ on the cross. She composed several books describing the inner sufferings of Christ, as well as offering spiritual instructions.

Baptista died on May 31, 1524, and was canonized in 2010.

A wonderful grace of the Holy Spirit led me into the depths of the heart of Jesus—an unfathomable sea of bitterness in which I should have been drowned had not God supported me.

—St. Baptista Varano

St. Thomas More

Martyr, Third Order Franciscan

(1478–1535)
· · · · · · · · ·

Thomas More was one of the most highly respected men of his time. A successful barrister, an honest judge, a famous scholar, he rose to the highest status of any commoner in England, appointed by Henry VIII to the office of lord chancellor.

More had little ambition for worldly success. As he later wrote, "Reputation, honor, fame, what is all that but a breath of air from another person's mouth no sooner spoken but gone? Thus whoever finds his delight in them is feeding on wind." More was a man of deep and demanding faith. In his youth he had considered a monastic vocation before discerning instead that he was called to serve God in the world. While outwardly he enjoyed a life of comfort, in the privacy of his spiritual life he wore a hair shirt, attended daily Mass, and practiced a strict discipline of prayer. He is believed to have become a Third Order Franciscan (and indeed his name is listed in the calendar of Franciscan saints).

More considered himself a loyal friend and servant of the king. But circumstances were to evolve to the point that Henry required a more absolute loyalty than More could offer. For some years Henry had been moving toward a fateful collision with the authority of the Catholic Church. The issue was his desire to annul his marriage to Catherine of Aragon to marry Anne Boleyn. When the pope blocked his way, Henry divorced Catherine, married Anne, and required that all subjects repudiate "any foreign authority, prince or potentate." Rather than oppose the king, More resigned his position, but when he refused to take the oath he was arrested and imprisoned in the Tower of London. The miseries of prison life, including cold, hunger, and vermin, were compounded by pressure from his family. When his wife tried to coax him to alter his course, he responded, "My good woman, you are no good at doing business. Do you really want me to exchange eternity for twenty years?"

After fifteen months, More was put on trial and convicted on the basis of perjured testimony. Now, with his fate settled, he at last broke his silence. He denied that Parliament had the authority to set up a temporal lord as head of the Church. He prayed, "that though your lordships have now here on earth been judges of my condemnation, we may yet hereafter in heaven merrily all meet together to everlasting salvation."

On the day of his execution on July 6, 1535, he displayed his characteristic wit, asking for the executioner's help in ascending the scaffold: "As for my coming down, let me shift for myself." Addressing the gathered crowd, he spoke: "I die in and for the faith of the holy Catholic Church. Pray for me in this world, and I shall pray for you in that world. Pray for the king that it please God to send him good counselors. I die as the king's true servant, but God's first."

Thomas More was canonized in 1935. In 2000, he was declared "the heavenly patron of statesmen and politicians."

Little as I meddle in the conscience of others, I am certain that my conscience belongs to me alone. It is the last thing that a man can do for his salvation: to be at one with himself.

—St. Thomas More

St. Angela Merici

Founder of the Ursulines, Third Order Franciscan

(1474–1540)

· · · · · · · · ·

Born in Lombardy and orphaned at an early age, Angela Merici became a Franciscan tertiary and embraced a life of prayerful simplicity. After spending many years in almost continuous pilgrimage, visiting the shrines of Italy, she had a vision one day in which she beheld a company of angels and maidens descending from a ladder in the heavens. A voice revealed that she would found a community whose members would be as numerous as the maidens thus revealed to her.

For some years Angela offered religious instruction to the children of her poor neighbors. Over the years, when not traveling, she had made this her regular occupation. Other women were gradually inspired to join her. Finally, after she had settled in Brescia, Angela had a group of twenty-eight women prepared to consecrate themselves with her to God's service. They chose as their patron St. Ursula, a legendary fourth-century martyr widely venerated as a protector of women.

Although she devised a simple rule for her Ursuline community, Angela did not initially conceive of them as a religious order. While dedicating themselves to the education of poor girls, the members wore no habits and took no vows; they continued to live with their families rather than behind an enclosure. The idea of such an association of religious women was unheard of at the time. But the work of Angela and her companions was widely admired. Angela observed, "Each member of the Company should strive to despoil herself of everything and set all her good, her love, her delight, not in robes, nor in food, nor in relatives, but in God alone and in his benign and ineffable Providence."

By the time of her death on January 27, 1540, Angela was revered as a living saint in Brescia. Crowds of people would follow her to church, attracted in part by her reputation for levitating several inches off the ground while gazing on the Eucharist. Four years after Angela's death, Rome approved a constitution for her congregation, which would in time come to number many tens of thousands. She was canonized in 1807.

Do now what you'll wish you had done when your moment comes to die.

—St. Angela Merici

꧁ ☩ ꧂

ST. PETER OF ALCÁNTARA
Franciscan Friar of the Stricter Observance
(1499–1562)
· · · · · · · · · ·

St. Peter, who was born in Alcántara, a small town in Spain, studied at the great university of Salamanca, and entered the Franciscans at the age of sixteen. From the start, Peter adopted a habit of extreme austerity. He trained himself to sleep no more than two hours a night; he wore no sandals on his feet; he would eat no flesh and drink no wine. Eventually he won permission to found a group of Franciscans along these lines. It was said that their cells—only seven feet long— resembled more graves than rooms. Nevertheless, he found many willing followers.

In the course of extensive preaching tours, he came to know St. Teresa of Avila and became her spiritual advisor. At that time she was seeking courage to undertake her reform of the Carmelite Order and she later testified on behalf of his canon- ization that it was Peter, more than anyone, who had encour- aged her mission. "When I came to know him he was very old, and his body so shriveled and weak that it seemed to be composed as it were of the roots and dried bark of a tree rather than flesh," she wrote. She also claimed, after his death in 1562, to receive visions of Peter, so that "Our Lord has been pleased to let me enjoy more of him than I did when he was alive."

One time a brother was complaining to Peter about the wickedness of the world, and the saint replied, "The remedy is simple. You and I must first be what we ought to be; then we shall have cured what concerns ourselves. Let each one do the same, and all will be well. The trouble is that we all talk of reforming others without ever reforming ourselves."

St. Peter died on October 18, 1562. He was canonized in 1669.

❧ ☩ ❧

I rejoiced at the things that were said to me: We shall go into the house of the Lord.

—FINAL WORDS OF ST. PETER OF ALCÁNTARA

⋐⋔⋑

St. Felix of Cantalice
Capuchin Friar
(1515–1587)
· · · · · · · · ·

St. Felix was born to a peasant family in Cantalice. When he was twelve, he was hired out as a shepherd and plowman. He found such work conducive to meditation. A turning point in his life came when the team of oxen he was driving suddenly bolted, knocking him down and pulling the sharp plow across his body. When he found himself completely unharmed, he determined at once to present himself for admission as a lay brother at the local Capuchin monastery of Città Ducale.

Very quickly, Felix acquired a reputation for holiness. Even members of his community referred to him as "the saint." After making his final vows, he was sent to Rome, where he lived for forty years, serving as the community's official beggar for food and alms. People called him "Brother Deo Gratias," for his habit of constantly giving thanks to God. Among his friends was St. Philip Neri, who read aloud to the illiterate brother the proposed rule for his new order and afterward incorporated his comments and amendments.

Felix was well known for his austerity. He walked barefoot, lived on little more than bread crusts and table scraps, and was later found to have worn a shirt of iron links. If anyone insulted him he would reply, "I pray God that you may become a saint!" He died on May 18, 1587, after receiving a vision of Our Lady. He was canonized in 1712.

෴

All earthly creatures can lift us up to God if we know how to look at them with an eye that is single.

—St. Felix of Cantalice

⊰⟐⊱

St. Benedict the Black
Franciscan Friar
(CA. 1526–1589)
· · · · · · · · · · · ·

St. Benedict was the son of African slaves, owned by a rich family in Sicily. Set free as a child, Benedict attracted attention, even as a youth, for his patience and charity. Once, as he was being taunted on account of his color, a passing Franciscan noticed him and invited him to join his community of hermits. Benedict did this. Eventually, in light of his evident holiness, he was chosen to serve as superior of the community.

In time, this informal group was directed by the pope to affiliate with a regular order. They joined the Order of Friars Minor. Benedict was accepted as a lay brother and put to work as a cook. Once again, however, his special gifts drew wonder and respect. Though he was illiterate, he had an extraordinary knowledge of Scripture and theology, and his gift for reading souls put him in great demand as a spiritual director. Eventually his fame became a form of penance, as the sick flocked to him for healing, and pilgrims of every station sought his counsel.

Benedict died in 1589 at the age of sixty-three. He was canonized in 1807. Apart from widespread veneration in Latin America, St. Benedict was claimed as a patron saint of African Americans.

There's a sweet, sweet Spirit in this place.

—FROM THE CORNERSTONE OF ST. BENEDICT THE
AFRICAN PARISH IN CHICAGO

⨳⨁⨳

St. Paschal Baylon

Franciscan Friar

(1540–1592)

· · · · · · · · ·

St. Paschal, who was born in Spain, spent his early life as a shepherd. Though he had no formal education, he taught himself to read and write, and he enjoyed the long days and nights with his flock, which afforded hours of uninterrupted prayer. At the age of twenty-one, he applied for admission to a friary of reformed Franciscans of St. Peter of Alcántara, a community known for its strict poverty and austerity. Paschal adapted happily to this environment, assigned mostly to menial tasks and joining his brothers in care for the poor and sick.

What distinguished Paschal was his extraordinary devotion to the Eucharist. He would spend hours each night or early morning on his knees before the Blessed Sacrament. Often he volunteered to serve at one Mass after another. Even while he lived he was known as "the saint of the Eucharist." And later, long after his death, he would be named the patron of all Eucharistic congresses and confraternities of the Blessed Sacrament.

On one occasion, Paschal was sent on a mission to France carrying letters for the minister general of the Observant Franciscans. It was a dangerous undertaking to cross Huguenot territory in his Franciscan garb, and several times he was stoned and severely injured. Nevertheless, he returned safely to resume his simple life. He died on May 17, 1592, at the age of fifty-two. He was canonized in 1690.

❦

I was born poor and am resolved to die in poverty and penance.

—St. Paschal Baylon

St. Francis Solano

Franciscan Friar

(1549–1610)

· · · · · · · · · ·

Francis Solano was born in the Andalusian town of Montilla, where he joined the Franciscans in 1569. While ministering in southern Spain, he cared for the victims of plague, a most perilous undertaking. At one point, he himself nearly died of the disease. Though he wished to be assigned to Africa, in 1589 Francis was sent to Peru. Along the way, a fierce storm drove his ship onto a sandbar close to shore. While the rest of the crew abandoned ship, leaving behind a cargo of African slaves, Francis chose to remain behind. Three days later, when the weather cleared, the survivors were rescued.

For his achievements over the next twenty years, Francis became known as the "Wonderworker of the New World." Venturing into the remote region of Tucamán, in present-day Argentina and Paraguay, he went out to meet the Indians, announcing his arrival with the sound of his violin. He was gifted in learning the indigenous languages—so much so that he was reputed to have a "gift of tongues." But though his gentleness won the Indians' affection, his efforts to protect them from Spanish exploitation had only mixed results.

Later he was assigned to Lima. There, his preaching against corruption and injustice caused such an uproar that his

superiors pleaded with him to moderate his speech. He died on
July 14, 1610, having uttered his last words: "Glory be to God."
He was canonized in 1726.

⤳ ✦ ⤶

God chose Francis Solano to be the hope and edifica-
tion of all Peru, the example and glory of Lima, the
splendor of the Seraphic order.

—FROM THE FUNERAL ORATION FOR
ST. FRANCIS SOLANO

༺ ✟ ༻

St. Fidelis of Sigmaringen
Capuchin Martyr
(1577–1622)
. . . .

For years, Mark Roy sought success as a lawyer, before disillusionment over the dishonesty rampant in his profession inspired him to pursue religious life. Upon entering the Capuchin Franciscans of Freiburg, he received the name "Fidelis"—faithful. Following his ordination, he proved zealous in his commitment to prayer and poverty, and threw himself ardently into pastoral work. As he wrote, "Woe betide me if I should prove to be a half-hearted soldier in the service of my thorn-crowned captain."

In 1622, he was assigned to lead a missionary team under the newly formed Congregation for the Propagation of the Faith to preach in Calvinist territories in Switzerland. It was an exceptionally dangerous mission. He set out armed only with a Crucifix, a Bible, a breviary, and a copy of the Capuchin Rule.

He preached widely, but his presence provoked outrage among many Calvinists. Apart from religious differences, they saw in the Capuchins an advance guard of Austrian intervention. In truth, Fidelis sometimes traveled under the protection of Austrian soldiers. Still, he faced beatings, rock-throwing, and in one case, a musket fired in his direction as he was saying Mass. Anticipating his fate, he signed his letters, "Father Fidelis, soon to become food for worms."

On April 24, after preaching in the church of Seewis, he was confronted by a Calvinist mob, demanding that he renounce his faith. "The Catholic religion is the faith of all ages," he replied. "I fear not death." He was felled by a single blow to his head and died instantly. St. Fidelis was canonized in 1729.

Lord, forgive my enemies. They do not know what they are doing. Lord Jesus, have mercy on me! Holy Mary, my Mother, help me!

—Last words of St. Fidelis

☙ ✠ ☚

BLESSED JOHN OF PRADO
Franciscan Martyr
(D. CA. 1631)
· · · · · · · · · ·

John of Prado was born to a noble family in Spain. After studies at Salamanca University he became an Observant Franciscan. Though he wished to pursue mission work in North Africa, his superiors instead gave him preaching assignments at home. He filled various offices in his order, though at one time he was removed from office on account of some unfounded accusation. After his eventual vindication, he was given a new assignment as minister of the province of San Diego.

A number of Franciscans at the time were working in Morocco, particularly among Christian slaves. When they all died during an outbreak of plague, John asked permission to take their place. After being named apostolic missionary by Pope Urban VIII, he set off with two companions. In Morocco, he managed to gain access to the Christian slaves and ministered to them, bolstering their faith and providing the sacraments. When his activities were discovered, he was imprisoned in chains and forced to turn a grindstone. Brought before the sultan, he proclaimed his faith and refused to apostatize. After being scourged, he was again returned for examination. This time, John began to preach to the audience, which included a number of Christian apostates. This enraged the sultan, who struck him to the ground and ordered his execution. He was burned alive in the public square, all the while singing Christ's praises.

John of Prado was beatified in 1728.

❦

God wills that I should suffer. May His will be done.

—Blessed John of Prado

BLESSED JOHN BAPTIST BULLAKER

Franciscan Priest and Martyr

(1604–1642)

· · · · · · · · · ·

John Baptist Bullaker was born in Chichester, England. When he was eighteen, he resolved to become a missionary priest. All Catholic institutions in England at this point having been suppressed, he went to France and studied at the Jesuit College at St. Omer. The next year, he entered the Franciscans.

After his ordination in 1628, he prepared to return to England, a most dangerous mission territory. Any priest found on English soil was subject to arrest; the same was true for those who harbored him. In fact, Bullaker was arrested immediately upon his landing, though after several months in jail he was released for lack of evidence. Thus, he was able to carry on a clandestine ministry for fourteen years, mostly among the gentry. Holing up in hidden cupboards, traveling in disguise, he was passed from house to house, saying Mass, hearing confessions, comforting the faithful, attending to the sick and dying, while managing to evade the authorities and their watchful spies. Finally, on September 11, 1642, he was betrayed by a maid in a house where he was saying Mass, and arrested.

Asked by the sheriff his purpose in returning to England, he answered, "to bring back my country to the fold of Christ from which it was gone astray." Tried and convicted of treason, he was sentenced to death. On October 12, he was hanged in Tyburn before a large crowd. While still alive, he was disemboweled, then quartered; his head was displayed on London Bridge.

Along with other English martyrs, he was beatified by Pope John Paul II in 1989.

❦

Then the Recorder said, Mr. Bullaker, you have here confessed over and over again that you are a priest, plead therefore to your indictment directly, guilty or not guilty. I answered as before, I am not guilty of any treason, but a priest I am.

—Blessed John Baptist Bullaker

St. Mariana of Quito
Third Order Franciscan
(1618–1645)
· · · · · · · · ·

Mariana de Paredes, the patron saint of Ecuador, was born in Quito to aristocratic parents. As a child, she dreamed of joining a convent, or even carrying the Gospel to Japan. But after her parents died, she moved in with her sister and brother-in-law, and there, under the direction of a Jesuit confessor, spent the rest of her life. Upon receiving the habit of a Franciscan tertiary, she took the name Mariana of Jesus.

It is painful to read of the austerities she imposed on herself: extreme fasting, long vigils, and a crown of thorns. As a reminder of death, she spent each Friday night sleeping in a coffin. In exchange for these sacrifices, she received many spiritual favors, including the gift of prophecy and the power to effect miraculous healings.

In 1645, Quito was struck by a series of earthquakes, followed by a terrible epidemic that claimed over fourteen hundred lives. When a preacher proclaimed that these sufferings were a result of the people's sins, Mariana publicly offered herself as a victim. Immediately the earthquakes ceased. But Mariana fell mortally ill and died on May 26, 1645, at the age of twenty-six. Hailed as the savior of her city, she was mourned by all of Quito. She was canonized in 1950.

❧ ✠ ❧

We are dealing with one who is, in a certain sense, like the final phrase of a symphony, which gathers up all of the themes, taking from each one something characteristic, to put together the marvelous harmony of spirit.

—POPE PIUS XII ON ST. MARIANA

St. Joseph of Cupertino
Franciscan Mystic
(1603–1663)
· · · · · · · · · ·

St. Joseph was born to a poor family in the small Italian town of Cupertino. His early life offered no evidence of any special gifts. He was considered slow-witted and easily distracted. He made several unsuccessful attempts to become a Franciscan before winning acceptance as a servant by the Conventual Franciscans at Tortella. There he received the habit of a tertiary, and was set to work in the stables. Though he remained a poor student—he could barely read and write—he won respect for his humility and deep faith. He was admitted as a novice, and eventually (by a stroke of luck in his examination), he was ordained as a priest.

From this point, Joseph began to display extraordinary spiritual gifts. At the thought of any holy mystery, he would be transported into a state of ecstasy. On such occasions, he would be visibly transported into the air. These levitations were documented by many reputable witnesses. While his reputation began to attract wide attention, his fits of "giddiness" aroused the suspicion of Church officials, who charged that he was "feigning holiness" and setting himself up as a "new messiah." Joseph was repeatedly called before the Inquisition and even brought to meet with the pope. He was cleared of any charges.

Nevertheless, he was ordered not to say Mass in public, and ultimately he was assigned to a series of secluded friaries, forbidden to have any dealings with the outside world.

Joseph died on June 12, 1656. He was canonized in 1767.

They feel as though they were taken into a wonderful gallery, shining with never-ending beauty, where in a glass, with a single look, they apprehend the marvelous vision which God is pleased to show them.

—St. Joseph of Cupertino, when asked what the souls in ecstasy behold

Venerable Maria of Jesus of Agreda
Franciscan Abbess and Mystic
(1602–1665)
. . . .

Maria of Jesus spent her entire life within the confines of her family castle in Agreda, Spain, which her mother—when Maria was only twelve—had converted into a convent for herself and her daughters. In this Franciscan Convent of the Immaculate Conception of Agreda, Maria eventually served as abbess, renowned for her mystical writings and her ardor in prayer.

And yet, in the spiritual realm, she was anything but a stay-at-home nun. In her early twenties, she found herself repeatedly transported in prayer to the Indian settlements in New Spain, particularly to a tribe of hunter-gatherers called the Jumanos in present-day New Mexico. In the course of what she reckoned were five hundred trips, she was able to communicate with the Indians in their own language, instructing them in the faith, and urging them to seek baptism. This remarkable story gained credence when friars in New Spain encountered just such a tribe who requested baptism and claimed they had met frequently with a Lady in Blue (just like Maria).

These reports were taken seriously enough to justify a trip to Agreda by the Franciscan superior for New Mexico. Maria was also subjected to two inquiries by the Inquisition, resulting in no action. (Her defenders included King Philip IV of Spain.)

She died on May 24, 1665. Ten years later, she was declared venerable by Pope Clement X.

My heart never delighted in earthly things, for they did not fill the emptiness in my spirit. For this reason, the world died for me in my youngest years, before I really came to know it.

—Venerable Maria of Jesus of Agreda

St. Bernard of Corleone
Capuchin Friar
(1605–1667)
· · · · · · · · ·

Filippo Latino, the son of a shoemaker in the town of Corleone, trained as a soldier and earned a reputation as the greatest swordsman in Sicily. Equipped with a hot temper, he was evidently quick to draw his blade. This was the cause of his conversion.

One day, in a public altercation, he seriously wounded a policeman and fled to a nearby Capuchin friary to seek sanctuary. His refuge extended for a number of days, during which time he seriously examined his life. Eventually he resolved to enter the Capuchins as a lay brother and became known as Brother Bernard.

His zeal for prayer and for self-sacrifice were widely recognized, and he acquired a reputation for miracles—particularly his ability to heal animals. This generally followed his saying the Lord's Prayer over the suffering creature, after which he would lead it three times around a cross in front of the friary. "How could I do otherwise?" he explained. The animals could not speak for themselves and had no doctors to attend to them.

Brother Bernard died on January 12, 1667. He was canonized in 2001.

Paradise! Paradise! Paradise! O, blessed are the disci-plines, blissful the night-watches! Blessed the penances, the self-will sacrificed! O, the blessing of fasting, and acts of obedience! How great is the blessing of religious life well lived!

—LAST WORDS OF ST. BERNARD OF CORLEONE

St. Pedro de San José Betancur
*Third Order Franciscan, Founder of the
Hospitaler Bethlemites*
(1619–1667)
· · · · · · · · ·

St. Pedro de San José Betancur is sometimes called the "Saint Francis of the Americas." Born in the Canary Islands, he spent his youth as a shepherd. At thirty-one, he traveled to Guatemala but arrived so impoverished that he relied on a Franciscan breadline for subsistence. Hoping to become a priest, he enrolled in a Jesuit college, though academic studies did not suit him. He soon withdrew and instead became a Franciscan tertiary.

Pedro devoted himself to the works of mercy, establishing a hospital—Our Lady of Bethlehem—as well as a hostel, a school, chapels, and other charitable institutes, which he supported by begging in the streets. When young men sought to join him he founded a new order, the Hospitaler Bethlemites.

Devotion to the Holy Family played a central role in his spirituality. He is credited with having originated the *Posada* celebrations that remain popular to this day in Mexico and Central America. On Christmas Eve, a man and woman, representing Mary and Joseph, lead a procession in search of shelter in Bethlehem. Wherever this custom is observed, it offers a reminder that the best way to honor the Holy Family and the birth of Christ is to extend charity and hospitality toward those in need.

Pedro died on April 25, 1667. Canonized in 2002, he became the first saint of Guatemala.

❧ ✣ ☙

Brother Pedro was a man of deep prayer who sought assiduously the will of God in each moment.

—POPE JOHN PAUL II ON ST. PEDRO DE SAN JOSÉ BETANCUR

ANGELUS SILESIUS
Franciscan Mystic and Poet
(1624–1677)
· · · · · · · · · ·

Johann Scheffler (his given name), was born to Protestant parents in Breslau, the capital of Silesia. After earning a doctorate in medicine, he served as court physician to Count Sylvius Nimrod, an ardent Lutheran. Over time, his public questioning of Lutheran doctrine and his increasingly mystical leanings caused him to be viewed with suspicion. In 1653, he resigned from his position, converted to Catholicism, and took the name Angelus Silesius. After joining the Franciscans, he was ordained a priest.

Silesius is best remembered for his two volumes of mystical poetry, *The Soul's Spiritual Delight* and *The Cherubic Pilgrim.* Most of his poems consist of epigrammatic rhyming couplets— many later adapted by both Catholic and Protestant hymnists. Silesius was fascinated by the relation between God and creation, the divine and the soul:

> A Loaf holds many grains of corn
> And many myriad drops the Sea:
> So is God's Oneness Multitude
> And that great Multitude are we.

His ability to detect God's presence in all things caused some to accuse him of pantheism. But he did not worship nature.

Instead, he saw in all creation the outflowing of divine love and energy and believed that the same energy and love was drawing all things toward final reunion with God.

The All proceedeth from the One,

And into One must All regress:

If otherwise, the All remains

Asunder-riven manyness.

Silesius died on July 9, 1677.

All heaven's glory is within and so is hell's fierce burning. You must yourself decide in which direction you are turning.

—Angelus Silesius

Venerable Antonio Margil
Franciscan Missionary
(1657–1726)
· · · · · · · · ·

Antonio Margil was born in Valencia, Spain. At a young age, he entered the Franciscans and adopted the nickname "Nothingness Itself," by which he subsequently signed his letters. At twenty-five, after distinguishing himself as a preacher and theologian, he was ordained. Immediately, he volunteered to join the mission in New Spain.

Fr. Antonio spent many years as a missionary in Yucatan, Costa Rica, and Guatemala. Always traveling on foot, he overcame the fears of the Indians by his poverty and simplicity, and his determination to dissociate himself from Spanish rule. For some time he interrupted his travels to preside over a missionary college in Zacatecas in Mexico, then traveled north to participate in a missionary expedition to Texas. There he established six missions, including the mission of San Antonio. His reputation for holiness began to grow, fed by astonishment over his ability to traverse huge distances in no time, to read people's souls, and other miraculous signs. Above all, he was renowned for his charity. As he said, "We must serve our neighbor more than ourselves, for by so doing we make Almighty God our debtor, and He will aid us in our necessities."

Eventually he returned to Mexico, where he died on August

6, 1726. In 1836 Pope Gregory XVI issued a decree of his heroic virtues, and he was declared venerable.

To enjoy God there is an eternity given to us; but to perform some service for God and to do some good to our brethren, the time for that is very short.

—Venerable Antonio Margil

St. Veronica Giuliani
Capuchin Abbess
(1660–1727)
· · · · · · · · ·

Ursula Giuliani was born in the small Italian town of Mercatello. At the age of seventeen, after receiving a vision of the Blessed Mother, she entered the Capuchin convent of Città di Castello in Umbria, and took the name Veronica. Early in her religious life, she began to experience an extraordinary identification with the Passion of Christ. In 1694, she displayed on her forehead the imprint of the crown of thorns. In one vision, she saw the crucified Christ remove his arm from the cross and beckon to embrace her by his side. As she felt an arrow pierce her heart and received on her body the wounds of the crucifixion, she wrote, "I felt great pain but in this same pain I saw myself, I felt myself, totally transformed into God."

Veronica's physical wounds were examined and treated by medical professionals, with no effect. After a personal examination by the bishop, he ordered that her hands be covered in gloves and sealed with his personal seal. She was to be deprived of the Eucharist, kept away from the other nuns, and subjected to constant supervision. But when her signs nevertheless continued, she was allowed to resume her regular life.

Despite her extraordinary mystical gifts, there was nothing unbalanced about Veronica's religious life. She served for thirty years as novice mistress and spent her last ten years as abbess of her convent. She died on July 9, 1727, and was canonized in 1839.

I have found Love, Love has let himself be seen!

—Last words of St. Veronica Giuliani

St. Leonard of Port Maurice
Franciscan Friar
(1676–1751)
· · · · · · · · · ·

St. Leonard, who was born in Port Maurice in Italy, joined the Franciscans when he was twenty-one, hoping to spend his life preaching the Gospel in China. In the end, his mission field did not extend beyond Italy. Nevertheless, Alphonsus Liguori called him "the great missionary of the eighteenth century."

A gifted preacher, he conducted mission tours through Umbria, Genoa, and the Marches. Enormous crowds would turn out to hear him—so great that he would preach in the open air. Wherever he went, his preaching prompted a spiritual revival. One of his favorite "preaching aids" was the Stations of the Cross—a devotion he was largely responsible for popularizing. It is said that he established 571 Stations throughout Italy, even in the Colosseum in Rome. He also promoted devotion to the Sacred Heart and was an early advocate for defining the dogma of Mary's Immaculate Conception.

In 1744, Pope Benedict XIV sent him on a mission to Corsica—one of his less successful undertakings, as many people assumed he was an agent of the ruling doge of Genoa. Shaking the dust from his feet, he resumed his work in Italy, preaching and leading retreats. By that time, however, his energy was failing fast.

He died in Rome on November 26, 1751. He was canonized in 1867.

❧ ✠ ❧

> If the Lord at the moment of my death reproves me for being too kind to sinners, I will answer, "My dear Jesus, if it is a fault to be too kind to sinners, it is a fault I learned from you, for you never scolded anyone who came to you seeking mercy."
>
> —St. Leonard of Port Maurice

St. Mary Crescentia

Third Order Regular Franciscan

(1682–1744)

· · · · · · · · ·

Anna Höss, the daughter of poor weavers, was born in a small town in Bavaria. While praying in the chapel of a local convent of Third Order Franciscans, she seemed to hear a voice from the crucifix saying, "This shall be your home." Unfortunately, the convent refused to accept her, for she lacked the required dowry. Nevertheless, when she was twenty-one, the Protestant mayor of the town, who had done favors for the convent, interceded with the nuns to accept her as a postulant. She took the name Mary Crescentia.

Her first years in the convent were filled with trials. The other nuns resented Mary, calling her a beggar, assigning her the most menial tasks, and forcing her to sleep in a corner on the floor. She accepted these ordeals with humility. In time, under a new superior, her virtues were recognized. She was accepted as a full member of the community and was steadily entrusted with positions of increasing responsibility: portress, novice mistress, and eventually mother superior. Through her wisdom and prayer, she carried the community to new heights of devotion, and her reputation spread beyond the convent.

After her death on April 5, 1744, her tomb became a popular pilgrimage site. She was canonized by Pope John Paul II in 2001.

The practices most pleasing to God are those which he himself imposes—to bear meekly and patiently the adversities he sends or which our neighbors inflict on us.

—St. Mary Crescentia

⌘

St. Ignatius of Laconi
Capuchin Friar
(1700–1781)
· · · · · · · · · ·

Francis Ignatius Vincent was born to a large family in
the village of Laconi in Sardinia. He was a frail child and
during one bout of illness his mother vowed, should he recover,
that she would give him to the Franciscans. When he did rally,
his father balked at fulfilling this pledge. "Today or tomorrow,"
he reasoned, "this year or the next, it all comes to the same
thing." But Francis would not be deterred from his vocation.
When he was twenty-one, he applied to the Capuchins and
received the name Brother Ignatius.

Ignatius spent most of his life in obscure and humble assignments. He had no special talents, save his extraordinary apti-
tude for begging. This became the principal occupation of his
life. People proved exceptionally happy to give him alms, and
in exchange he often reconciled feuding neighbors, reformed
sinners, or left a trail of miraculous healings.

There was in town a notorious moneylender whom Ignatius
never approached. The moneylender took offense at this ostra-
cism and complained to the Capuchin superior, who subsequently instructed Ignatius to include this man on his rounds.
Ignatius complied with this command, and he returned that
evening with a bag filled with food. But when he opened it up

it was dripping with blood. "What is this?" asked the superior. "Father Guardian," Ignatius replied, "this is the blood of the poor. And that is why I ask nothing from that house."

Ignatius died on May 11, 1781. He was canonized in 1951.

❦

Trust God.

—Favorite motto of St. Ignatius of Laconi

❧✢❧

St. Benedict Joseph Labre
Third Order Franciscan
(1748–1783)
· · · · · · · · ·

Benedict Joseph Labre was born to a large family in a village in northern France. When he was twelve, his family sent him to live with an uncle, a parish priest. There he received some rudimentary education. When his uncle died, Benedict decided to devote his life to God. He was turned away from the Trappists and a series of other religious communities. Discouraged, he divined that his true vocation was to seek a cloister within the world. After becoming a Third Order Franciscan, he set off on foot on a pilgrimage that lasted several years, wandering thousands of miles across Europe, all the while praying and visiting shrines.

Benedict dressed in rags and never bathed, a habit that discouraged human contact. He declined to beg but accepted alms. When no food was offered, he lived off what was discarded on the road. His appearance evoked as much contempt as pity. But those who were able to see beneath his appearance—including, eventually, his confessor—recognized the saint in their midst.

In time, Benedict settled in Rome, where he spent his nights in the ruins of the Colosseum and his days praying in the churches of the city. At the age of thirty-five, he collapsed and died on April 16, 1783. Almost immediately, children of the neighborhood began calling through the streets, "The saint is dead, the saint is dead!" His reputation quickly spread. Biographies were published. One of these made its way to his village, where his astonished parents learned what had become of their long-lost son. He was canonized in 1883.

I am only a poor, ignorant beggar.

—St. Benedict Joseph Labre

֍

St. Junipero Serra
Franciscan Missionary
(1713–1784)
· · · · · · · · ·

Junipero Serra is celebrated as one of the fathers of California. Born in Majorca, Serra entered the Franciscan order at sixteen. After earning a doctorate in theology, he taught as a professor for many years before volunteering for the missions in New Spain. He spent twenty years in Mexico, then traveled by foot to California, where he spent the rest of his life. From his arrival in 1769, when he founded the mission of San Diego, until his death fifteen years later, he tirelessly traveled the length of California, established nine missions, and baptized many thousands of Indians.

Serra espoused an austere, ascetic brand of Catholicism. In preaching, he was capable of demonstrating his zeal by striking his breast with a stone, or holding a lighted torch against his chest to demonstrate the fires of hell.

His canonization in 2015—the first to take place on North American soil—was not without controversy. Critics, including many Native Americans, raised questions about the mission settlements in which Indian converts were incorporated, becoming virtual prisoners or indentured servants. Others defended Serra and the Franciscan missionaries for protecting the Indians from harsher abuse by the secular authorities.

Serra died on August 28, 1784. He is buried in the sanctuary floor of the Mission de San Carlos Borromeo in Carmel.

⟪✢⟫

What I should like to be able to do is to affix to their hearts the words, "Put you on the Lord Jesus Christ." May the most provident Lord and heavenly Father grant that my wish be accomplished in their regard.

—St. Junipero Serra

ᜡᜡ

St. Mary-Magdalen Postel
Founder, Poor Daughters of Mercy
(1756–1846)
• • • • • • • • •

Julia Frances Catherine Postel was born in a small French town near Cherbourg. After studying in a Benedictine convent, she returned home to teach school, though privately she dedicated herself to God's service. Her calling became clear, with the onset of the Revolution, when her parish priest was forced to go underground. Postel put herself at his service, setting up a secret chapel in her home, where clandestine services could be conducted. She herself undertook religious duties, such as carrying consecrated Hosts to administer to the dying. Thus, as Pope Pius X later commented, she served as a veritable "maiden priest."

As the persecution receded, Postel devoted herself to repairing the local church, offering religious instruction, organizing prayer guilds, and performing works of mercy. In 1807, she determined that what she really wanted to do was to teach children, and for this she should organize a religious congregation. She joined with three companions in taking religious vows. Observing the rule of the Third Order of St. Francis, they called themselves the Poor Daughters of Mercy. She became Mother Mary-Magdalen.

Thirty years later, their motherhouse was transferred from

Cherbourg to a former Benedictine abbey in Courtance. Their new bishop urged them to replace their former rule with that of St. John Baptist de la Salle, and they changed their name to the Sisters of the Christian Schools of Mercy. After the order struggled for some years of dire poverty, the bishop urged them to disband. But Mother Mary-Magdalen persisted, and eventually their fortunes turned.

She died on July 16, 1846 at the age of eighty-nine. She was canonized in 1925.

⁂

I want to teach the young and to inspire them with the love of God and liking for work. I want to help the poor and relieve them of some of their misery. These are the things I want to do.

—St. Mary-Magdalen Postel

༺༗༻

MOTHER MARY FRANCIS BACHMANN

Founder, Sisters of St. Francis of Philadelphia

(1824–1863)

· · · · · · · · ·

Anna Maria Boll Bachmann, who was born in Bavaria, immigrated to the United States and settled in Philadelphia. In 1851, when her husband Anthony was killed in an accident in a stone quarry, she found herself a widow with three young children and a fourth on the way. To support herself, she and her sister opened a small hostel for immigrant women. In time, they conceived the idea of joining a religious community. Their confessor, a Redemptorist priest, encouraged them in the direction of the Third Order Franciscans and wrote to Bishop John Neumann, then in Rome, on their behalf. This overture was well timed. Bishop Neumann had been seeking help from the pope in securing German Dominican sisters to help in his diocese. But the pope had encouraged him instead to start a local Franciscan community. Thus, on his return, he provided instruction to Anna, her sister, and another woman who had joined them, and accepted them into religious life. In 1855, the Franciscan Sisters of Philadelphia was established, with Anna, now Mother Mary Francis, as superior.

The sisters supported themselves by sewing and alms, while initially caring for immigrant women. Eventually, Bishop Neumann steered them into wider ministries: a school, an orphanage, and even a hospital for the sick poor. The latter undertaking followed their work in caring for the poor during an outbreak of smallpox, when no other hospital in the city would accept patients with contagious diseases.

Mother Mary Francis died of tuberculosis on June 30, 1863.

We feed so many who come to the door. As long as God does not stop giving to us we shall not stop giving to the poor.

—MOTHER MARY FRANCIS BACHMANN

༺ ☙ ༻

BLESSED MARIANO ROCCACASALE

Franciscan Friar

(1778–1866)

· · · · · · · · ·

Mariano was born to a peasant family in Roccacasale in Italy. One day, tired and thirsty while caring for his sheep on a rugged hillside, he fell asleep and had a dream in which a Franciscan friar showed him where to find water. When he awoke, he removed a stone beneath his head, untapping a vigorous stream, which runs to this day.

When he was twenty-three, he joined a Franciscan community in Arisquia, where he remained for twelve years, dividing his time between prayer and simple labor. But he felt something was lacking. Eventually he received permission from his community to visit Bellagra, where many holy friars had established hermitages. He ended up remaining there for the next forty years, serving as doorkeeper—an office that afforded opportunities to greet pilgrims, travelers, and the poor who made their way to his door. Welcoming each guest with the Franciscan greeting, "Peace and Good," he would offer food, a place to rest, and his own spiritual counsel. This was his path to holiness.

He died on May 31, 1866. He was beatified in 1999.

❧ ⚜ ☙

Regarding the life and spirituality of Blessed Mariano of Roccacasale, Franciscan religious…. His life of poverty and humility, following in the footsteps of St. Francis and St. Clare of Assisi, was constantly directed toward his neighbors in the desire to listen to and share the troubles of every one of them, in order to present them later to the Lord in his long hours of prayer before the Eucharist.

—Pope John Paul II

St. Clelia Barbieri

Founder, Minims of Our Lady of Sorrows

(1847–1870)

· · · · · · · · · ·

Clelia Barbieri was born in 1847 to a poor family on the outskirts of Bologna. After her father's death, when she was eight, she went to work spinning hemp. Despite her own modest circumstances, Clelia sought every opportunity to serve her neighbors. She became well known in her parish for teaching catechism and encouraging other young girls in their faith. During this time, she conceived the idea of gathering a household of other young women who would devote themselves to prayer and good works. With support from their parish priest, they took over an abandoned house and implemented this vision. Neighbors arrived the first night with donations of food. Clelia remarked, "I like the idea that our house resembles the crib where the shepherds bring their gifts."

Clelia and her companions endured poverty and hardship. In time, their community took the form of a new congregation, the Minims of Our Lady of Sorrows, under the patronage of St. Francis of Paola. Clelia devised a rule that emphasized community, the spirit of contemplation, the practice of charity, simplicity, and joy. But her years were limited. She succumbed to tuberculosis at twenty-three, dying on July 13, 1870. She was canonized in 1989.

O great Lord God, You see that my will is to love You and to try to avoid offending You. O Lord, open Your heart and throw out the flames of love. Enkindle my heart with these flames and burn me with love.

—St. Clelia Barbieri

Blessed Frances Schervier

Founder, Sisters of the Poor of St. Francis

(1819–1876)

· · · · · · · · · ·

Frances Schervier, the daughter of a wealthy industrialist, was born in Aachen. Upon the death of her mother when Frances was thirteen, the young girl assumed responsibility for the household and the care of her younger siblings. With other women in Aachen she engaged in various charitable projects, visiting prisoners, caring for the sick in their homes, and rescuing prostitutes. In 1844, she entered the Third Order of St. Francis.

In 1845, following the death of her father, she joined with several other women to form a religious community, the Sisters of the Poor of St. Francis. They established soup kitchens and fearlessly cared for those suffering from typhoid, cholera, and smallpox. Eventually, Frances sent sisters to America, where she visited in 1863 and offered her services as a nurse during the Civil War. Returning to Germany, she joined her sisters in nursing soldiers and staffing ambulances during the Franco-Prussian War.

She died on December 14, 1876. Her beatification followed in 1974.

❧ ✠ ❧

If we do this [follow Jesus's command to love one another] faithfully and zealously, we will experience the truth of the words of our father St. Francis who says that love lightens all difficulties and sweetens all bitterness. We will likewise partake of the blessing which St. Francis promised to all his children, both present and future, after having admonished them to love one another even as he had loved them and continues to love them.

—Blessed Frances Schervier

⚜

St. Maria Josepha Rossello
Founder, Daughters of Our Lady of Mercy
(1811–1880)
· · · · · · · · ·

Benedetta Rossello was born to a large, poor family on the Ligurian coast of Italy. Lack of a dowry frustrated her desire to enter religious life. Instead she became a Third Order Franciscan and entered domestic service to a wealthy family, sending all her earnings to her family.

When she heard that the bishop of Savona wished to do something for girls and young women at risk of abuse, she volunteered her services. The bishop recognized her gifts and readily agreed to set her up with three companions in a run-down house. They took the name Daughters of Our Lady of Mercy, and Benedetta, who would serve as superior for the rest of her life, became Maria Josepha.

Despite their poverty, they quickly attracted new recruits. Remembering her own sad experience, Mother Maria decreed that no worthy woman should be turned away for lack of a dowry. At first, the sisters founded a series of homes—Houses of Divine Providence—for girls in trouble. But schools and hospitals followed, and in 1875, the first foundation was established in Argentina.

Mother Maria never scorned the most humble tasks. But when illness left her unable to walk, she could do no more than oversee the work of her sisters. "There are God, the soul, eternity," she said, "the rest is nothing." She died on December 7, 1880. She was canonized in 1949.

The hands are made for work, and the heart for God.

—St. Maria Josepha Rossello

꧁ ֍ ꧂

Blessed María del Tránsito Cabanillas

Founder, Franciscan Tertiary Missionaries

(1821–1885)

· · · · · · · · ·

Eugenia de los Dolores, to use her baptismal name, was born in Cordoba in Argentina. Drawn from an early age to religious life, she dreamed of starting a religious institute for the care of poor and abandoned children. Her path, however, was convoluted. Starting as a Franciscan tertiary, she was persuaded to join a Carmelite convent. When her health failed, she left and joined a convent of the Visitandine Sisters. This too proved too rigorous for her constitution.

Finally, with support from a Franciscan priest, she returned to her original plan. With two companions, she founded the Franciscan Tertiary Missionaries of Argentina, dedicated to providing religious education for poor children. Her congregation flourished.

Maria died on August 25, 1885. She was declared blessed in 2002, becoming the first Argentinean woman to be beatified.

The flame that burned in her heart brought María del Tránsito to seek intimacy with Christ in the contemplative life.... The Franciscan ideal then appeared as the true way God wanted for her, and...she undertook a life of poverty, humility, patience and charity, giving rise to a new religious family.

—POPE JOHN PAUL II

Robert Ellsberg

Blessed Mary Catherine of Cairo

Founder, Franciscan Missionary Sisters

(1813–1887)

· · · · · · · · · ·

Constanza Troiani was born in Italy in 1813. At the age of six, following her mother's death, she was entrusted to the Franciscan Sisters of Ferentino. At sixteen, in the convent in which she was raised, she was accepted as a novice, taking the name Sr. Mary Catherine of St. Rose of Viterbo.

Many years passed. One day, a visiting priest just back from Egypt spoke of the need for sisters in Cairo. Mary Catherine, who had always yearned to be a missionary, won permission from her convent to accept this challenge and with five other sisters departed for Cairo. Once there—the first Italian sisters in Egypt—they set about learning Arabic and embarked on care for the poor, opening an orphanage that welcomed children of all races and religious backgrounds.

Yet, her convent had considered this a temporary mission, and when the sisters were instructed to return, they faced a dilemma. Choosing to sever ties with their congregation, they received permission from Rome to establish a new congregation: the Franciscan Missionary Sisters of Egypt. Along with their previous work, Mother Mary Catherine, known widely as "Mother of the Poor," fearlessly took up the antislavery cause. Asked by a sister during an outbreak of cholera whether anything frightened her, she replied, "My dear, only a lack of faith frightens me."

Her passing, on May 6, 1887, was mourned throughout Cairo by Christians and Muslims alike. She was beatified in 1985.

The will of God is my perpetual hunger, my thirst, and my yearning.

—BLESSED MARY CATHERINE OF CAIRO

MOTHER MARY IGNATIUS HAYES
Founder, Missionary Franciscan Sisters
of the Immaculate Conception
(1823–1894)
· · · · · · · · · ·

Elizabeth Hayes, the daughter of an Anglican priest, pursued a circuitous spiritual journey. Starting out in an Anglican religious community in Oxford, she converted to Catholicism and later joined a Franciscan community in Greenwich. Aside from the traditional three religious vows, she took a fourth—to make herself available to the needs of mission. Her subsequent journey led her to Jamaica, then France, and finally to Belle Prairie, Minnesota, at that time a remote outpost. Operating out of a log cabin with a small group of sisters, she formed the Missionary Franciscan Sisters of the Immaculate Conception.

They faced enormous hurdles. At one point, Mother Mary Ignatius Hayes, as she was now known, traveled to Italy, hoping to find other Franciscans willing to join her in the prairie. She returned alone. But, eventually, her community grew and she decided it was time to spread out—this time to serve the African American community in the South. In 1879, she established a new community in Georgia, providing education to the children of recently freed slaves.

The next year, she traveled to Rome for an audience with Pope Leo XIII. He persuaded her to open a novitiate in Rome. She complied, though it meant she would never return to the United States. She died on May 6, 1894.

※ ✝ ※

The greatest miracle is myself, that I should be a Catholic, a religious, a Franciscan. Yet, I am so weak bodily, so sensitive mentally, that left to myself a moment I should not bear up against the least cross.

— MOTHER MARY IGNATIUS HAYES

BLESSED ANGELA TRUSZKOWSKA

Third Order Franciscan, Founder of the Felician Sisters

(1825–1899)
· · · · · · · · ·

Camille Sophia Truszkowska, who later took the religious name Mother Angela, was born in Poland to an educated, middle-class family. Her father, who was a juvenile court judge, encouraged Camille's acute social conscience and her interest in uncovering the causes of poverty and injustice. At the age of twenty-three, she underwent what she called her "conversion," the beginning of an intense life of prayer and devotion. Though she considered entering a contemplative order, she perceived that her vocation was to be of service to the suffering poor. Joining the St. Vincent de Paul Society, she spent her time visiting and befriending those on the margins. At the suggestion of her spiritual director, a Capuchin priest, she joined the Third Order of St. Francis.

In 1855, she and a companion took a vow before the icon of Our Lady, pledging themselves to the will of God in all things. This became the foundation of the Sisters of St. Felix, a name inspired by a local Franciscan shrine. The works of the congregation, the first in Poland to combine action and contemplation, were wide-ranging, involving care for orphans, social centers, and hospitals.

At the age of forty-four, Mother Angela retired from leadership and quietly devoted herself to prayer. She lived on for thirty years, much of the time suffering in poor health. Her community, meanwhile, continued to grow, even sending sisters to North America. She died on October 10, 1899. She was beatified by Pope John Paul II in 1993.

Do not discriminate among the sick. Give aid to all without exception; your vocation obliges you not to exclude anyone, for everybody is your neighbor.

—Blessed Angela Truszkowska

֎ ✿ ֎

BLESSED ANNA ROSA GATTORNO

Third Order Franciscan, Founder, Daughters of St. Ann

(1831–1900)

· · · · · · · · · ·

Benedetta Gattorno was born in Genoa to a wealthy family. Married at twenty-one, she was widowed six years later, with two young children to care for—one of them deaf and mute. Despite these challenges, she underwent what she called a "conversion" to greater love of God and her neighbors. Already a daily communicant, she took private vows of chastity and obedience, later adding poverty when she became a Franciscan tertiary.

Her confessor urged her to establish a religious congregation, but she worried about what would happen to her children. In this, she received encouragement from Pope Pius IX. During an audience, he reassured her that God would provide for her children. And so, in 1866, she founded the Daughters of St. Anne (named for the mother of Mary), and later took the name Anna Rosa. The mission of the sisters was to be "Servants of the poor and ministers of mercy," seeking out and responding to all forms of suffering—whether among the poor, the abandoned, orphans, the sick, or elderly. She took a special interest in deaf children.

In 1878, the first sisters left Italy to establish houses in Latin America and other parts of Europe. By the time of Anna Rosa's death on May 6, 1900, there were thirty-five hundred sisters at work in over three hundred houses. She was beatified in 2000.

Although I am in the midst of such a torrent of things to do, I am never without the union with my God.

—Blessed Anna Rosa Gattorno

༺༒༻

St. Hermina Grivot
Franciscan Martyr
(1866–1900)
· · · · · · · · ·

As a young woman in Burgundy, Hermina Grivot joined a missionary congregation, the Franciscan Sisters of Mary, hoping to be sent overseas, praying for the grace to become a saint, worrying only that the time of martyrdom had probably passed.

In 1898, the missionary bishop of Shanxi province asked her community for a contingent of sisters to staff an orphanage and dispensary in Taiyuan, China. Grivot was happy to be put in charge of this mission. The next year, she and her sisters embarked on the long and arduous journey to China. They were ill-prepared for what faced them—knowing not a word of Chinese, and having no particular training in education or nursing. Even the priests in the mission did not speak the language, but relied on translators. Nevertheless, they all energetically rose to meet the enormous challenges at hand.

As it turned out, they had arrived at a perilous time. Rising nationalist resentments over foreign exploitation were about to ignite in the Boxer Rebellion of 1900. The uprising targeted Europeans and Chinese converts to Christianity—Christianity being seen by many Chinese as a tool of colonialism.

On July 9, a large number of Franciscan missionaries in Taiyuan, including Bishop Gregory Grassi and the entire cohort of sisters, were arrested. Grassi had urged the sisters to dress in Chinese clothes, but they had refused: "Don't stop us from dying with you," they replied. They were all beheaded, Sister Hermina among them. She was canonized in 2000.

Adoration of the Blessed Sacrament is half my life. The other half consists in loving Jesus and winning souls for Him.

— St. Hermina Grivot

༺ ༀ ༻

BLESSED CONTARDO FERRINI
Third Order Franciscan
(1859–1902)
· · · · · · · · ·

Among the great majority of official saints drawn from traditional "religious life," Contardo Ferrini stands out as a layman who lived out his faith in the world of scholarship and civic service. From his early youth he displayed a deep dedication to prayer. But rather than enter the priesthood, he chose the academic life as his own path to holiness. Through studies in Pavia in Italy, and later in Berlin, he became one of the world's authorities on Roman law. He taught at a number of universities and published hundreds of scholarly articles and several textbooks. In 1895, he was elected to the municipal council of Milan. Apart from this work he had a passion for nature and mountaineering.

Although he was a Franciscan tertiary, he was not the type of saint famous for exceptional acts of charity or mystical visions. What seems to have impressed those who came in contact with him was an overwhelming goodness and thirst for life — the evidence that it is possible to lead a holy life in the midst of the ordinary duties of work and life in the world.

In pronouncing his beatification in 1947, Pope Pius XII referred to him as a man who "gave an emphatic 'Yes' to the possibility of holiness in these days."

Ferrini died of typhus on October 17, 1902, at the age of forty-three.

❧✠❧

Nature lives by the breath of God's omnipotence, smiles in its joy of him, hides from his wrath—yet greets him, eternally young, with the smile of its own youth.

—Blessed Contardo Ferrini

⊂⊃⊹⊂⊃

BLESSED MARY OF THE PASSION
Founder, Franciscan Missionaries of Mary
(1839–1904)
· · · · · · · · · ·

Hélène Marie Philippine was born in France to a noble family. After a short stint with the Poor Clares she joined a contemplative community in Toulouse, the Society of Mary Reparatrix, where she took the name Mary of the Passion. In 1865, she was sent to Madurai in southern India, where her order was helping to establish a congregation of Indian sisters. There she proved so adept in leadership that she was named provincial superior. In 1876, however, long-simmering divisions in the community erupted to the point that Mary and nineteen other sisters withdrew and established a community under the aegis of the Paris Foreign Mission Society.

At this point, Mary conceived of a new congregation that would combine contemplation with active mission work. After becoming a Third Order Franciscan, she received permission from Rome to establish the Franciscan Missionaries of Mary. Her community grew with impressive speed. In India, she directed her sisters to provide medical care for women, whose health was compromised by their unwillingness to be seen by male doctors.

Mary's sisters spread across the world, often in perilous situations. Seven of them (later canonized) were killed in China during the Boxer Rebellion. Mary remained the superior general until her death on November 15, 1904, at which time there were over two thousand Franciscan Missionaries of Mary working in eighty-six countries. She was beatified in 2002.

Combining a mystical and an active vocation, passionate and intrepid, she gave herself with an intuitive and bold readiness to the universal mission of the Church.

—POPE JOHN PAUL II

❧❀❧

BLESSED MARIA THERESIA BONZEL

Founder, Sisters of St. Francis of Perpetual Adoration

(1830–1905)

· · · · · · · · · ·

Regina Christine Wilhelmine Bonzel was born in Germany to a deeply religious family. Early in life, she felt the call to religious life. She recalled:

On the day of my First Holy Communion, I was unspeakably happy. Before that I was a vivacious child, ready to take part in every prank. But after I received the Lord in my heart and returned to my place, an indescribable feeling came over me. Without really knowing what I was saying, I repeated over and over again, "O Lord, I am your victim, accept me as your victim; do not reject me."

Her parents refused to allow her to enter a religious order, but when she was twenty, she entered the Third Order of St. Francis. With a group of friends she embarked on a life of service to orphans. Eventually, they were recognized as a new congregation, the Sisters of St. Francis of Perpetual Adoration. She became superior, taking the name Maria Theresia. As new members joined them, the order established a series of schools, hospitals, and orphanages. She was determined that her sisters always embrace the spirit of poverty, humility, and charity.

"We are children of St. Francis," she said. "We must follow his example."

During the Franco-Prussian War, Mother Maria's sisters cared for over eight hundred wounded soldiers. Yet, after the war, the government instituted a series of harsh anti-Catholic measures known as the Kulturkampf. Severe restrictions were placed on all religious congregations, and the sisters were forbidden to accept new members. Mother Maria responded by sending sisters to Indiana in the United States. She herself accompanied the first six missionaries in 1875, and returned twice more to oversee their expanding work.

Mother Maria died on February 6, 1905. She was beatified in 2013.

All as God wishes. He leads, I follow.

—BLESSED MARIA THERESIA BONZEL

಼ྋಬ

BLESSED MARIA ASSUNTA PALLOTTA

Franciscan Missionaries of Mary

(1878–1905)

· · · · · · · · ·

Maria Assunta Pallotta was born to a working-class family in Italy. By the time she was eleven, she was helping to support her siblings. But all the while, she dreamed of a religious vocation. When she was in her late teens, with support from her parish priest, she entered the Franciscan Missionaries of Mary, traveling to the motherhouse in Rome. There, and in subsequent assignments, she joyfully embraced all duties, no matter how menial. She was especially happy to be assigned to farm work, caring for chickens, goats, and pigs. In a letter to her parents, she explained her sense of mission: "I ask the Lord for the grace to make known to the world purity of intention—which consists in doing everything for the love of God, even the most ordinary actions."

Eventually, she would travel to the far side of the earth. It was only a few years since several members of her order in China had faced martyrdom during the Boxer uprising. Maria was eager to replace them. In February 1904, soon after taking her final vows, she received the joyous confirmation of her new assignment. Almost immediately, she departed for China, arriving during a particularly extreme winter. Yet only a year later, she was stricken with typhus. She died on April 7, 1905.

In 1954, she became the first non-martyr missionary sister to be beatified.

֎

What God wills, as He wills, and may
His Will be done.

—BLESSED MARIA ASSUNTA PALLOTTA

༺ ༓ ༻

Venerable Mary Magdalen Bentivoglio
Poor Clare
(1834–1905)
• • • • • • • • • •

In October 1875, Sr. Mary Magdalen Bentivoglio and her sister Constance, with whom she had entered the Poor Clares, sailed from Italy to New York to establish the first contemplative community in the United States. They had departed with the personal blessings of Pope Pius IX, who urged them to offer "a silent sermon accompanied by prayer and union with God, to make known to many that true happiness is not to be found in things temporal and material."

Unfortunately, they had departed with no assurance of a welcome. Not knowing a word of English, they were left to beg and rely on charity for most of a year while seeking a bishop who would accept them. The bishop of New York told them that a contemplative enclosure was out of character with the American spirit; the need was for teaching sisters. After fruitless efforts in other cities, the two sisters were finally welcomed by the bishop of Omaha, and they made their home in that diocese.

For years, they suffered cold and hunger. As Mother Mary Magdalen wrote, "It is certain that on the one hand we do not want to pamper anyone, but on the other hand we do not want to kill anyone." But new postulants did arrive, and in time

Mother Mary Magdalen traveled to establish a new foundation in Evansville, Indiana, where she lived until her death on August 18, 1905.

All my life I have asked God for crosses and now that He has sent them, why should I not be glad?

—VENERABLE MARY MAGDALEN BENTIVOGLIO

❧❦❧

St. Albert Chmielowski
Third Order Franciscan, Founder of the
Albertine Brothers and Sisters
(1845–1916)
· · · · · · · · · ·

Adam Chmielowski was born in Poland to an aristocratic family. At seventeen, he lost a leg while participating in a nationalist uprising. Afterward, he was drawn to art and began to enjoy recognition for his painting. At the same time, living in Krakow, his heart was increasingly moved by the sufferings of the poor. He finally gave up his life as an artist to assume the life of a poor beggar. With the name Brother Albert, he donned a gray robe and became a Third Order Franciscan.

In time he founded orders of men and women, known as the Albertine Brothers and Sisters, who practiced the works of mercy in soup kitchens and homeless shelters. In one of the shelters that he founded, Brother Albert died on Christmas Day, 1916.

His reputation lived on. Among the priests who attributed their vocation to his example was Karol Wojtyla, who in 1949 wrote a play about him. Years later, as Pope John Paul II, he championed Albert's cause and later presided over both his beatification and, in 1989, his canonization. He said of St. Albert, "In his tireless, heroic service on behalf of the marginalized and the poor, he ultimately found his path. He found

Christ. He took upon himself Christ's yoke and burden; he did not become merely 'one of those who give alms,' but became the brother to those he served."

❧ ✠ ☙

You must be as good as bread, which for everyone rests on the table and from which everyone, if hungry, may cut himself a piece for nourishment.

—St. Albert Chmielowski

St. Marianne Cope

Third Order Regular, Servant of the Lepers

(1838–1918)

· · · · · · · · ·

Barbara Koob, who was born in Germany, immigrated with her family to the United States when she was less than two years old. At the port of entry, the family name became Cope. In 1862, Barbara entered the Third Order Regular of Franciscans and received her religious name, Sr. Marianne. Her early years were spent teaching in her order's schools and later serving as administrator of a hospital. In 1883, now the superior general of her congregation, she received a request from King Kalakaua in Hawaii for help in caring for leprosy patients. Though fifty other congregations had already declined the king's plea, Mother Marianne responded at once: "I am hungry for the work and I wish with all my heart to be one of the chosen Ones, whose privilege it will be to sacrifice them-selves for the salvation of the souls of the poor Islanders."

That year, she and six sisters sailed for Hawaii and imme-diately set to work establishing a hospital in Maui. Given the general fear of contagion and the social stigma attached to those suffering from Hansen's disease, the sisters' dedication to their patients won wide respect. Eventually, Mother Marianne consented to move to the island of Molokai, where the most serious cases were confined. There, one of her first tasks was to care for Fr. Damien de Veuster, the famous "Apostle to the Lepers," who had succumbed to the disease during his long years of service. She embraced her work with joy: "Should I live a thousand years I could not in ever so small a degree thank Him for His gifts and blessings…. I do not expect a high place in Heaven—I shall be thankful for a little corner where I may love God for all eternity."

Apart from nursing her patients, Mother Marianne strove to create an atmosphere of beauty and peace. Planting flowers around the hospital, she transformed the barren landscape into a garden.

Mother Marianne died of natural causes on August 9, 1918. She was canonized in 2012.

❧ ⚜ ☙

Let us make best use of the fleeting moments. They will not return.

—St. Marianne Cope

⌒⌒⋔⌒⌒

BLESSED ANGELA SALAWA
Third Order Franciscan
(1881–1922)
· · · · · · · · · ·

Angela Salawa was born to a poor family in Krakow, Poland. At the age of sixteen, she found work as a maid and lived a carefree and worldly life. A turning point came as she was dancing during a wedding reception and suddenly perceived that Christ was standing in the room, seeming to hold her in a gaze of loving reproach. Immediately she went to a nearby church, where she prayed for the courage to amend her life. Rather than enter a religious order, she decided to pursue a life of prayer and service in the world. In 1912, she became a Third Order Franciscan.

With the outbreak of World War I, Krakow was evacuated, but Angela chose to remain, nursing soldiers and prisoners of war while offering comfort to all who suffered. In her diary, she wrote to Christ: "I want you to be adored as much as you were destroyed." Her own health suffered, but no one noticed. In 1916, she was fired by her employer, who accused her of stealing. Penniless and without other resources, she lived out her last years in a basement room, where she died alone on March 12, 1922, at the age of forty.

Despite her obscurity, her reputation for holiness endured beyond her death. She was beatified in 1991 by Pope John Paul II.

❧❦❧

Lord, I live by your will. I shall die when you desire; save me because you can.

—Blessed Angela Salawa

Venerable Matt Talbot
Third Order Franciscan
(1856–1925)
. . . .

Matt Talbot was one of twelve children born to a poor family in Dublin. His addiction to alcohol began at twelve, when he got his first job with a wine merchant. Before long, drink had become the primary focus of his life. All the wages he earned carrying bricks went to support his addiction. What funds he lacked, he begged, borrowed, or stole.

This lasted until the age of twenty-eight, when he was overcome with disgust for his life. Entering a church, he made his confession and took the pledge of abstinence for three months. His mother had cautioned him: "Go, in God's name, but don't take it unless you are going to keep it." Those first three months were agonizing. At one point he collapsed on the steps of a church, in despair at the thought of breaking his oath. But he kept at it, renewed it for another three months, and thus, by constant vigilance, remained sober for the next forty-one years.

From the point that he took the pledge, the focus of his life shifted dramatically. He became a Franciscan tertiary, attended daily Mass, ate sparingly, prayed half the night, and gave generously to charity. (He never carried money with him—always fearful of the temptation to step into a pub.)

On June 7, 1925, Talbot collapsed in the street and died. It was discovered that his body was wrapped in penitential chains, which were buried with him. His cause for canonization was soon opened, and in 1975 he was declared venerable. He is the patron of alcoholics.

Three things I cannot escape: the eye of God, the voice of conscience, the stroke of death. In company, guard your tongue. In your family, guard your temper. When alone, guard your thoughts.

—Venerable Matt Talbot

Venerable Margaret Sinclair
Poor Clare
(1900–1925)
· · · · · · · · ·

Margaret Sinclair was born in Edinburgh to a poor family. She left school at fourteen to work in a series of factories, helping to support her family. An eventual marriage proposal served as the catalyst for deeper reflection on her vocation, resulting in her decision to enter the Poor Clares. As the community in Edinburgh had no room for her, she was accepted into a community in Notting Hill in London. She was given the name Sister Mary Frances of the Five Wounds.

Her working-class roots and her Scottish brogue set her apart from the educated and upper-class backgrounds of the other sisters. One time, noticing that Margaret was having too much fun whitewashing an outhouse, a nun upbraided her, "You'll never be a saint." Margaret replied, *"Dinna fash yerself"* (Don't let that trouble you).

Her time in the convent was limited. She died of tuberculosis on November 24, 1925, at the age of twenty-five. Her last words were the prayer, "Jesus, Mary and Joseph, I give you my heart and my soul."

Despite her obscure life, her reputation soon spread, especially in Scotland, where she was celebrated as a saint of ordinary life. The archbishop of Edinburgh said, "We can still admire the heroism of the early martyrs, but the unlikelihood of our being thrown to the lions makes these first Christian saints somewhat remote and shadowy figures. Margaret Sinclair may well be one of the first to achieve the title of Saint from the factory floor."

She was declared venerable in 1978. Pope John Paul II described her as "one of God's little ones who, through her very simplicity, was touched by God with a real holiness of life."

O, God…I desire to…rejoice when I feel the pinch of poverty, and always remain modest and prudent, thinking of this in our Blessed Lady, and how she would like it in her child.

—Venerable Margaret Sinclair

EVE LAVALLIERE
Third Order Franciscan
(1866–1929)
· · · · · · · · · ·

For years, Eve Lavalliere was the toast of Parisian society, a famous beauty and the most popular actress on the French stage. While performing for royalty across Europe, she enjoyed the favors of numerous lovers. "I had everything the world could offer," she noted, "everything I could desire. Nevertheless, I regarded myself as the unhappiest of souls." Unhappiness ran deep in life. Her abominable childhood had ended the day her father, in a drunken rage, shot her mother and then killed himself. Her later fame and wealth could not fill the void.

And yet Eve's life took a dramatic turn in 1917 when a priest gave her a biography of Mary Magdalene and challenged her to read it. At first defiantly, and then with tears of remorse, she read the book, and when she had finished she resolved to make her peace with God. "My resolution is made," Eve wrote. "From now on, only Jesus has a right to my life, for He alone gave me happiness and peace."

Abandoning her glittering life, Eve first sought to enter religious life, but she was rejected by a number of convents on account of her notoriety. Instead, she became a Third Order Franciscan. For several years, until ill health overtook her, she volunteered with a lay-missionary nursing order in Tunisia. She spent her last years alone, penniless, and in great suffering. Yet she insisted she was the "happiest person in the world." In her notebook she wrote, "I thank You, O my God, that You have given me shelter beneath your roof. Abandonment, love, trust—such is my motto." She died on July 10, 1929.

I left everything for God; He alone is enough.

—Inscription on the gravestone of Eve Lavalliere

༼ঔৣ৾ঔ༽

MOTHER THEODORE WILLIAMS

Founder, Handmaids of the Most Pure Heart of Mary

(1868–1931)

· · · · · · · · ·

Elizabeth Barbara Williams was born to a large Catholic family in Baton Rouge. Though she felt called to religious life, there were at the time few options available for an African American woman in the South. For some years she worked as a receptionist for a convent of white nuns. Then, in 1916, she was approached by a French priest, Fr. Ignatius Lissner, who was serving the black Catholic community in Savannah. At the time, laws were under consideration that would prevent white teachers, like the sisters in Lissner's parish school, from teaching black children. In response, Fr. Lissner wished to start a congregation of black sisters. In Williams, he found an enthusiastic partner. As Mother Theodore, Williams became the founder of the Handmaids of the Most Pure Heart of Mary.

When the proposed laws were not passed, the Handmaids found themselves struggling to find their mission. Though they were largely accepted in the community, they confronted doubts from certain white nuns. As Fr. Lissner noted, "As real Southerners they could not believe a colored woman could make a real Religious Sister….'It is a shame,' they said. 'Fr.

Lissner may give them the veil, but what will that prevent them from stealing chickens and telling lies?'"

Then, in 1923, Archbishop Patrick Hayes invited the Handmaids to relocate to Harlem. There, besides teaching, they operated a soup kitchen, a kindergarten, and a shelter for homeless children. In 1929, Williams affiliated her community with the Franciscans. She died on July 14, 1931.

God knows how many souls they reached.

—Fr. Ignatius Lissner on Mother Theodore and the Handmaids

Mother Lurana White

Founder, Franciscan Sisters of the Atonement

(1870–1935)

. . . .

Lurana White was raised in New York in a wealthy family of high church Episcopalians. While attending a boarding school run by an order of Episcopal sisters, she felt a strong attraction to religious life. With her family's permission, she entered the order as a postulant. She was pained, however, that her Episcopal order did not take a corporate vow of poverty. At this time, she heard about an Episcopal priest, Paul Watson, who was promoting reunion between the Anglican communion and Rome. Eventually they met and vowed to found a new Episcopal order in the spirit of St. Francis: the Society of the Atonement. Watson understood atonement both in the sense of redemption as well as *at-one-ment*—the cause of Christian unity. As founder of the Franciscan Sisters of the Atonement, White became Mother Lurana. She and Watson established a new home on a site named Graymoor in Garrison, New York.

Fr. Watson's enthusiasm for Rome faced increasing opposition within the Episcopal Church. Eventually, in 1909, he and Mother Lurana successfully petitioned the Vatican to accept their community into the Catholic Church.

The community grew rapidly. Graymoor became a center not only for retreats but also for hospitality to indigent people and the down-and-out. On one occasion, a priest came seeking the superior of the sisters. Dubious when Mother Lurana introduced herself, he protested that surely she was too young. She replied, "That is one fault of mine which will be remedied in time." She died on April 15, 1935.

I wished to do and suffer something worthwhile for God and for others.

—MOTHER LURANA WHITE

St. Maximilian Kolbe
Franciscan Martyr
(1894–1941)
· · · · · · · · ·

On July 30, 1941, a prisoner escaped from Auschwitz, the notorious Nazi camp in Poland. In retaliation, the commandant lined up inmates of cell block fourteen and ordered that ten of them be selected for death. When one of the ten cried out that he would never see his family again, another prisoner stepped forward and volunteered to take his place. When the commandant asked who he was, he replied, "I am a Catholic priest." His offer was accepted, and so Fr. Maximilian Kolbe assumed his place among the condemned.

Fr. Kolbe had entered the Franciscans at sixteen. Though a sickly youth, he was animated by pious zeal that was matched by a genius for organization. After his ordination, he formed a movement called the Knights of Mary Immaculate and launched a series of journals, which achieved a circulation of eight hundred thousand in Poland. He also organized a community called City of the Immaculate, which grew to include 762 Conventual friars, making it the largest religious community of men in the world. In the 1930s, he started a similar foundation in Japan.

He was back in Poland in 1939 when the Nazis invaded. Gauging the Nazis' enmity for religion, he intuited his eventual fate and prepared himself for a time of suffering. "I would like to suffer and die in a knightly manner," he stated, "even to the shedding of the last drop of my blood, to hasten the day of gaining the whole world for the Immaculate Mother of God." He was arrested in February 1941, and by May he was on his way to Auschwitz. He survived three months of labor and horrendous suffering. But his final passion began in July when he and the other prisoners were locked in a death bunker with nothing to consume but their own urine. He passed the time leading his companions in prayer, preparing them for death, and keeping vigil with them as they gradually succumbed. When, after two weeks, Kolbe and three others were still alive, the Nazis dispatched them with injections of carbolic acid.

In 1982, Pope John Paul II, who as bishop of Krakow had often prayed at the site of Kolbe's death, presided over his canonization in Rome. Present for the ceremony was the man whose life Kolbe had saved. The pope called Kolbe a true martyr and saint for our times whose heroic charity proved victorious over the architects of death.

⁊⚓⁊

These Nazis will not kill our souls, since we prisoners certainly distinguish ourselves quite definitely from our tormentors; they will not be able to deprive us of the dignity of our Catholic belief. We will not give up. And when we die, then we die pure and peaceful, resigned to God in our hearts.

—St. Maximilian Kolbe

Blessed Caritas Brader

Founder, Franciscan Sisters of Mary Immaculate

(1860–1943)
· · · · · · · · · ·

Maria Josefa Carolina Brader was born in Switzerland in 1860. At the age of twenty, she joined the cloistered Franciscan convent of Maria Hilf and took the name Sister Caritas. When a new disposition made it possible for cloistered nuns to engage in apostolic work, she volunteered for a mission to South America. Her superior happily endorsed this plan: "Sister Caritas," she wrote, "is supremely generous, shows no reluctance to any sacrifice, and with her extraordinary practical sense and education will be able to render great services to the mission."

In 1893, she arrived in Tuquerres, Colombia, along with six other sisters. They operated in a vast territory that encompassed tropical jungles, coastal areas, and Andean highlands. Eventually Sr. Caritas saw the need for a larger missionary order and received permission to found the Franciscan Sisters of Mary Immaculate, with a mission focused on education for the poor. As Superior General of the community, Mother Caritas encouraged her sisters to pursue higher education. "Do not forget," she told them, "that the better educated, the greater the skills the educator possesses, the more she will be able to do for our holy religion and the glory of God…. The more intense and visible her external activity, the deeper and more fervent her interior life must be."

She died on February 27, 1943, by which time her congregation had spread to many countries, including the United States. She was beatified in 2003.

❧ ☩ ❧

See God's will in everything, and do His will with joy, out of love of Him.

—Blessed Caritas Brader

⌘

BLESSED RESTITUTA KAFKA
Franciscan Sister, Martyr
(1894–1943)
· · · · · · · · ·

Restituta Kafka took her religious name from a third-century martyr beheaded under the Roman Emperor Aurelian, little guessing that the age of martyrdom had not passed. She was born in Vienna. At nineteen, she entered a nursing order, the Franciscan Sisters of Christian Charity, serving faithfully for many years in the district hospital in Mödling, near Vienna, where she was put in charge of the operating room.

After the Anschluss in 1938, the Nazis forbade any religious symbols in hospitals. Sr. Restituta not only refused to comply with this order, but she defiantly installed crucifixes in every room in a new ward of the hospital.

After being denounced to the Gestapo by a hospital surgeon, a fanatical Nazi, Sr. Restituta was arrested on Ash Wednesday in 1942. Martin Bormann, Hitler's private secretary, wished to make a special example of her and personally ordered her execution. After a year in prison, on March 30, 1943, she was beheaded. Her body was thrown into a mass grave.

Sr. Restituta was beatified by Pope John Paul II in 1998.

I have lived for Christ; I want to die for Christ.

—LAST WORDS OF BLESSED RESTITUTA KAFKA

∽҉∾

BLESSED FRANZ JÄGERSTÄTTER

Third Order Franciscan, Conscientious Objector and Martyr

(1907–1943)

· · · · · · · · · ·

Franz Jägerstätter, an Austrian peasant and devout Catholic, was executed for refusing to serve in Hitler's army. He was known in his village of St. Radegund as a man of honesty and principle, devoted to his family and his faith, a sacristan in his parish church, who in 1940 had joined the Third Order of St. Francis. He was also known as a fervent opponent of the Nazis—the only member of his village to vote against the 1938 Anschluss that incorporated Austria into "Greater Germany." Nevertheless, his singular act of resistance came as a surprise.

In 1943, when served with an induction notice, Franz turned himself in and announced his refusal to take a military oath. Before taking this stand he had sought counsel from his parish priest and even the local bishop. They had each advised him to do his duty and serve his Fatherland. But Franz believed the Nazis were a satanic movement and that any compromise would constitute a mortal sin.

In prison, he spurned ongoing appeals to save himself, convinced that he could not prolong his life at the price of his immortal soul. In this case, obedience to Christ meant disobedience to the state. But he took comfort in the knowledge that "not everything which the world considers a crime is a crime in the eyes of God. And I have every hope that I need not fear the eternal Judge because of this crime."

Franz was beheaded on August 9, 1943. For years, his story was little known beyond his family and fellow villagers. In time, however, his story spread, and he was recognized as a heroic witness to conscience. His sacrifice, seemingly fruitless in his own time, would illuminate the path of generations to come. He was beatified in 2007 in a ceremony attended by his widow and surviving children.

Neither prison nor chains nor sentence of death can rob a man of the Faith and his own free will. God gives so much strength that it is possible to bear any suffering, a strength far stronger than all the might of the world. The power of God cannot be overcome.

—Blessed Franz Jägerstätter

ᗑ ☩ ᗒ

BLESSED SOLANUS CASEY
Capuchin Friar
(1870–1957)
· · · · · · · · ·

Solanus Casey, the son of Irish immigrants in Wisconsin, felt called to the priesthood after witnessing a drunken sailor stabbing a woman. Somehow, this scene of sin and suffering caused Casey to dedicate himself to God and to promote God's love as the answer to the world's troubles. After entering the Capuchins, he was ordained a priest. But in light of his academic difficulties, his superiors placed restrictions on his priestly faculties. He was not permitted to hear confessions or preach on doctrine. Instead he spent most of his life as a porter at St. Bonaventure's monastery in Detroit and worked in the friars' soup kitchen.

Despite his humble office, Casey's extraordinary spiritual gifts were quickly recognized. A gifted reader of souls, he became particularly renowned for his ministry of healing prayer. Scores of people sought him out each day for spiritual counsel and intercession. Dutifully, he recorded their petitions in his prayer book and promised to ask God's assistance. Even in his lifetime, hundreds of miraculous cures were attributed to his prayers. In his final illness, he remarked, "I'm offering my suffering that all might be one. If only I could see the conversion of the whole world."

Since his death on July 31, 1957, at the age of eighty-six, the reports of healing miracles have continued unabated. In May 2017, one of these miracles was officially approved by Pope Francis, clearing the way for his beatification on November 18, 2017.

We must be faithful to the present moment or we will frustrate the plan of God for our lives.

—Blessed Solanus Casey

༄༅།

LOUIS MASSIGNON
Third Order Franciscan, Prophet of Dialogue
(1883–1962)
· · · · · · · · ·

Louis Massignon, a French scholar, played a key role in promoting the cause of Catholic-Muslim dialogue. The seeds of his vocation were planted in his youth and his avid interest in Arab culture. While conducting research in Mesopotamia he was arrested and charged as a spy. During his captivity, he received a profound mystical experience, which brought him to an overwhelming sense of God. This prompted an ardent return to his Catholic roots. But he was also deeply affected by the experience of Muslim piety and vowed to devote his life to increasing understanding between these two religious traditions, both heirs of the faith of Abraham. (He was also deeply influenced by his friendship with the desert hermit Blessed Charles de Foucauld.) In 1931 he became a Franciscan tertiary, taking the name "Ibrahim" (the Arabic form of Abraham).

A key point of reference for Massignon was God's visit to Abraham as a stranger in the form of three angels. By providing hospitality for God in our hearts, he wrote, "we enter the path of mystical union." He considered his encounter with Muslim spirituality (one of the three Abrahamic faiths) as a form of "sacred hospitality." At an abandoned Franciscan church in

Egypt where St. Francis had met Sultan al-Malik al-Kamil, Massignon made a vow, offering his life for the Muslims, "not so they would be converted, but so that the will of God might be accomplished in them and through them."

Later in life, Massignon became a Melkite Greek Catholic and was ordained a priest, permitting him to celebrate the Mass in Arabic according to the Byzantine Rite liturgy. A follower of Gandhian nonviolence, he supported efforts to promote peace in the Middle East and for a peaceful resolution of the war in Algeria. For the sake of sacred hospitality, he became an outspoken advocate for Muslim refugees in France.

He died on October 31, 1962.

Man is not made for works of external mercy, but first of all to worship the divine Guest in his heart, in the present moment.

—Louis Massignon

St. John XXIII

Pope, Third Order Franciscan

(1881–1963)

· · · · · · · · ·

On October 28, 1958, a new pope greeted the Church from the balcony overlooking St. Peter's Square. There stood the smiling, rotund figure of Angelo Giuseppe Roncalli, the son of peasants and recently the patriarch of Venice. "I am called John," he said.

In appearance, and in almost every other respect, Pope John XXIII stood in contrast with his gaunt and otherworldly predecessor, Pius XII. Gregarious and open, John exuded an enthusiasm for life that in itself set a positive tone for his pontificate and raised hopes for a season of change. These hopes were answered by the astonishing announcement that he intended to convene an ecumenical council, the first in almost a hundred years. He spoke of the need to "open the windows" of the Church and to let in fresh air. It was the signal of an extraordinary renewal, an era of openness and positive dialogue between the Church and the modern world.

On October 4, 1962, on the eve of the opening of the Second Vatican Council, Pope John made a rare trip outside of Rome to visit Assisi, to pray to the Blessed Mother and St. Francis for the success of the Council. It was a reminder of his deep Franciscan roots. As a young boy of fourteen, while enrolled in the junior seminary of Bergamo, he was received as a Third Order Franciscan. "Oh! The serene and innocent joy of that coincidence," he later said. "A Franciscan tertiary and cleric on his way to the priesthood, drawn in, therefore by the same cords of simplicity, still unconscious and happy, that was to accompany us up to the blessed altar that was later to give us everything in life."

There were many steps along the way to the Chair of St. Peter: Apostolic Visitor to Bulgaria and then Turkey, nuncio to France, and later Patriarch of Venice. But Pope John always acknowledged his familial bonds with the followers of St. Francis. In 1959, just after his election as pope, he presided over a celebration marking the 750th anniversary of Pope Innocent III's approval of the Franciscan Rule. At the end of his remarks, he said, "Beloved sons! Allow us to add a special word from the heart to all those here who belong to the peaceful army of the lay Tertiaries of St. Francis: I am your brother Joseph."

Having launched Vatican II, Pope John did not live to see it completed. Dying of cancer, he retained his humor and humility. "My bags are packed," he said, "and I am ready to go." From his deathbed he dictated a final message of hope for the Church he loved:

> Now more than ever, certainly more than in past centuries, our intention is to serve people as such and not only Catholics; to defend above all and everywhere the rights of the human person and not only those of the

Catholic Church; it is not the Gospel that changes; it is we who begin to understand it better.... The moment has arrived when we must recognize the signs of the times, seize the opportunity, and look far abroad.

Pope John XXIII died on June 3, 1963. In a few brief years he had won the hearts of the world, and his passing was universally mourned. He was canonized in April 2014.

⋘ ⚜ ⋙

In convening the Second Vatican Council, St. John XXIII showed an exquisite openness to the Holy Spirit. He let himself be led and he was for the Church a pastor, a servant-leader. This was his great service to the Church; he was the pope of openness to the Holy Spirit.

—POPE FRANCIS, AT THE CANONIZATION
OF ST. JOHN XXIII

❦

BLESSED MARIJA PETKOVIC
Founder, Daughters of Mercy
(1892–1966)
· · · · · · · · ·

Marija Petkovic was born to a poor family in southern Croatia. Committed to serving the poor, she entered a local convent of the Servants of Charity. Many of the sisters were Italian, and when, following the death of their superior, most of them decided to return to Italy, Marija was appointed by the bishop to serve as the new superior. He told her this meant being "the last among the Sisters, and if necessary going barefoot while the Sisters wore shoes…following the example of the crucified Jesus."

In 1920, she reestablished her community as a new congregation, the Daughters of Mercy, an independent Franciscan congregation with the mission of spreading knowledge of the love of God through performance of the works of mercy. She took the name Mary of Jesus Crucified.

Over time, she established forty-six communities, including several in Argentina. Her connection to Latin America contributed to the unusual miracle that was certified in approval of her beatification. In 1988, a trawler in the South Pacific crashed into a Peruvian submarine, which began to sink. An officer on board the submarine invoked the help of Marija Petkovic and reportedly received the strength to open a hatch against thousands of pounds of water pressure, allowing his crewmates to escape.

Marija Petkovic died on July 9, 1966. She was beatified in 2003.

Love infinitely the most sweet Lord Jesus Christ; do everything for him alone and spend your life in works of mercy and of love.

—BLESSED MARIJA PETKOVIC

꧁ ☘ ꧂

ST. PIO OF PIETRELCINA (PADRE PIO)
Capuchin Friar, Mystic
(1887–1968)
· · · · · · · · · ·

Padre Pio, a Capuchin friar of peasant background, spent virtually his entire life in a monastery in southern Italy. In most respects he was indistinguishable from his fellow friars. But for some mysterious purpose, Padre Pio was set apart. For the thousands of pilgrims who flocked to hear him say Mass, or to have him hear their confessions, or simply to rest their gaze on his bandaged hands, he was living proof for the existence of God.

Like his spiritual father St. Francis, Padre Pio was a stigmatic; he bore on his hands, feet, and side the wounds of Christ. These mysterious open wounds, for which there was no natural explanation, appeared on his body in 1910 and remained until some months before his death. He was credited with thousands of miracles and enjoyed other extraordinary gifts, including the ability to read the hearts of penitents. It was even said that he had the rare gift of bilocation—the ability to be in more than one place at the same time. In other words, he was endowed with a full repertoire of the supernatural gifts that once commonly adorned the lives of medieval saints. But this was a man living under the full glare of twentieth-century skepticism, an era when the miraculous was more likely to cause embarrassment than wonder.

He regarded his celebrity as a terrible cross. Many denounced him as a charlatan or a neurotic. To discourage his popularity, Church officials for many years instructed him not to say Mass. In part, this reflected a desire to discourage the cult of personality that surrounded Padre Pio, even during his life. At the same time, there was evidently a desire to discourage the notion that "miracles" *per se* are synonymous with holiness. Some suggested that Pio's wounds were a result of psychosomatic stress, caused by too much concentration on the passion of Christ. To this, Padre Pio responded, "Go out to the fields and look very closely at a bull. Concentrate on him with all your might. Do this and see if horns grown on your head!"

Eventually, his faith and sufferings were vindicated by the Church. In 2002, thirty-four years after his death in 1968, he was canonized by Pope John Paul II—formerly a Polish priest, Fr. Karol Wojtyla—whose papal election Padre Pio had prophesied in 1947 after hearing his confession.

❧ ⚜ ☙

I need to love You more and more, but I don't have any more love in my heart. I have given all my love to You. If You want more, fill my heart with Your love, and then oblige me to love You more and I will not refuse you.

—St. Pio of Pietrelcina

❦

VENERABLE MARTHE ROBIN
Third Order Franciscan, Founder of the Foyers of Charity
(1902–1981)
· · · · · · · · ·

Marthe Robin was born in 1902 in a small village near Lyons. Her early childhood was happy and unremarkable. When she was sixteen, however, she showed the first symptoms of a grave disease that would eventually leave her bedridden. On March 25, 1925, she offered a solemn prayer consecrating her life and her sufferings to God to help spread love in the world. Within three years she was totally paralyzed. That same year she entered the Franciscan Third Order. Unable to eat or drink, she was reportedly sustained for the rest of her life by the Eucharist alone. In time, she also received the marks of Christ's wounds on her hands and feet.

In 1936, a young priest named Georges Finet came to serve as her spiritual director. To him, she confided her vision for a new apostolic movement, the Foyers of Charity. With his help, her vision was realized. The Foyers of Charity is an international network of Catholic men and women who live, work, and pray together as a family to spread Christ's love in the world.

Marthe lived on for many years—blind and immobilized, yet active through her prayers in the life of the Church, dispensing spiritual counsel, and showing that even when a person is stripped of everything, she still has the power to love.

She died on February 6, 1981. In 2014, Pope Francis recognized her heroic virtues and she was declared venerable.

It seems to me that I am no more than a very tiny thing in the arms of God, and that I will remain so until I die…. I do not know what He wants to do with me, but I desire it all.

—Venerable Marthe Robin

❦

SERVANT OF GOD THEA BOWMAN
Franciscan Sister
(1937–1990)
· · · · · · · · · ·

Thea Bowman was one of the great treasures of the American Catholic Church. Ablaze with the spirit of love, the memory of struggle, and a faith in God's promises, she impressed her audiences not just with her message but also with the nobility of her spirit.

Born Bertha Bowman in rural Mississippi, she was baptized as a Catholic at the age of ten, while attending parochial school. Later, she was inspired to enter the congregation that ran her school, the Franciscan Sisters of Perpetual Adoration, and took the name Sister Thea. She found herself the only African American in a white religious order. But she had no desire to blend in. She believed her identity as a black woman entailed a special vocation; she was committed to asserting a black way of being Catholic. Thus, she believed the Church must make room for the spiritual traditions of African Americans, including the memory of slavery, but also the spirit of hope and resistance reflected in their spirituals, the importance of family, community, celebration, and remembrance.

"What does it mean to be black and Catholic?" she asked. "It means that I come to my church fully functioning. I bring myself, my black self, all that I am, all that I have, all that I hope to become. I bring my whole history, my traditions, my experience, my culture, my African-American song and dance and gesture and movement and teaching and preaching and healing and responsibility as gift to the Church."

She was a spellbinding speaker who preached the Gospel to audiences across the land, including the US bishops. In one speech, she noted that women were not allowed to preach in the Catholic Church. But this should not stop them from preaching everywhere else!

> God has called to us to speak the word that is Christ, that is truth, that is salvation. And if we speak that word in love and faith, with patience and prayer and perseverance, it will take root. It does have power to save us. Call one another! Testify! Teach! Act on the Word! Witness!

After being diagnosed with incurable cancer she bore a different kind of witness. She continued to travel and speak, even from her wheelchair. The faith that sustained the slaves, the hope expressed in the spirituals, the love embodied by St. Francis, now sustained her in her personal way of the cross. And to her other gifts to the Church she added the witness of her courage and trust in God. "I don't make sense of suffering. I try to make sense of life," she said. "I try each day to see God's will."

She died on March 30, 1990, at the age of fifty-two. Her cause for canonization is in process.

Maybe I'm not making big changes in the world, but if I have somehow helped or encouraged somebody along the journey then I've done what I'm called to do.

—Sr. Thea Bowman

꧁ ✿ ꧂

MARTYRS OF CHIMBOTE

(D. 1991)

· · · · · · ·

These martyrs are three priests, two Conventual Franciscans and an Italian missionary priest, murdered in August 1991 by the Shining Path guerrillas of Peru.

Alessandro Dordi, the eldest, was born in Italy in 1931. He had arrived in Peru in 1980. Michael Tomaszek, thirty-one, a Polish priest, had arrived in Peru in 1989, where he joined his fellow Franciscan, Zbigniew Adam Strzalkowski, thirty-three, who had arrived in 1988.

The two young priests were still struggling to learn Spanish, serving in a parish in the town of Pariocota, where they trained catechists, administered the sacraments, and served their neighbors in every way they could. Meanwhile the specter of the Shining Path was growing. This ultra-revolutionary movement targeted not only the authorities but also trade unionists, peasant leaders, and even whole villages that rejected their vision of pure communism. The priests were targeted as "enemies of the people," whose pastoral work undermined the thirst for revolution.

On August 9, 1991, the guerrillas attacked Pariocota, seized the two Polish priests, and shot them. When the news reached the neighboring parish of Fr. Dordi, he presumed that his own end was approaching. "Goodbye," he wrote to a friend, "I am going back now and they will kill me." He was murdered on August 25.

Officially recognized as martyrs, the three were beatified in December 2015.

I am a happy priest…. Overall, I am very well received.
I can feel it over and over, but this isn't so important to
me. I'm myself, and I want to be myself.

—FR. MICHAEL TOMASZEK

ᘓᑫᗢ

BLESSED DULCE PONTES

Founder, Workers Union of St. Francis

(1914–1992)

· · · · · · · · · ·

Maria Rita de Souza Pontes was born in Salvador, Brazil, to a well-to-do family. As a child, the sight of homeless beggars in her neighborhood inspired her to devote her life to the poor. At eighteen, she joined the Congregation of Missionary Sisters of the Immaculate Conception, a Franciscan community founded in Brazil in 1910. She took the religious name Dulce after her mother, who had died when Maria was just three years old.

Within a year of entering religious life, she had formed the Workers Union of St. Francis, the first Christian workers' movement in Brazil. Meanwhile she took to sheltering homeless sick people in abandoned houses, begging for food and medicine. As their numbers steadily increased, Dulce asked permission from her superior to house them in chicken sheds on the convent grounds. Eventually this gave rise to St. Anthony's Hospital, a complex of medical, educational, and social services. She could never pass a person in need without seeing the face of Christ: "We may be the last door, and for this reason we cannot close it." In 1959 Sister Dulce's various programs were consolidated as the Charitable Works Foundation of Sister Dulce (OSID).

Twice nominated for the Nobel Prize, Sister Dulce became one of the most beloved figures in Brazil. She died on March 13, 1992, and was beatified in 2011.

There is nothing better that you can do in this world than to totally give yourself to God in the person of the poor and our needy brother.

—BLESSED DULCE PONTES

FATHER DANIEL EGAN

"The Junkie Priest"

(1915–2000)

· · · · · · · · · ·

Daniel Egan, a Bronx native, joined the Franciscan Friars of the Atonement in 1935 and was ordained a priest. A turning point in his life came in 1952, as he was preaching in a church and noticed a woman in grave distress. She confessed that she was a drug addict struggling to kick her habit. Though Egan called every hospital in town, none would admit her: "She was shrugged off as a criminal." He decided at that moment that he must open a home for women like her. That was the inspiration for Village Haven, a halfway house for women addicts, located across the street from the women's house of detention.

The location was no accident. As Egan discovered, most of the women in the city jail were drug addicts. And yet few resources at the time were dedicated to recovery from addiction. Most authorities, even medical professionals, wrote off such addicts as hopeless cases. Fr. Egan believed otherwise.

Egan received permission from his order to dedicate himself full time to working with addicts, and he became such an expert in the field that he was dubbed "the Junkie Priest"—a name he happily adopted.

Fr. Egan died on February 10, 2000.

❧✦❧

If we had the vision of faith, we would see beneath every behavior—no matter how repulsive—beneath every bodily appearance—no matter how dirty or deformed—a priceless dignity and value that makes all material facts and scientific technologies fade into insignificance.

—FR. DANIEL EGAN

FATHER MYCHAL JUDGE
Franciscan Chaplain
(1933–2001)
· · · · · · · · ·

On the bright fall morning of September 11, 2001, fire-fighters across New York were summoned to a scene of unimaginable horror: Two hijacked airliners had crashed into the twin towers of the World Trade Center. As firefighters rushed into the burning buildings, they were accompanied by their chaplain, Fr. Mychal Judge. Hundreds of them would die that day, among the nearly three thousand fatalities in New York, Washington, and Pennsylvania. Fr. Judge would be among them.

In the days that followed, the story of his life and his sacrifice would become known around the world: how he had joined the Franciscans at the age of fifteen, how he had acquired a wide reputation for his ministry among the poor and home-less, alcoholics, and people with AIDS, and his outreach to the gay community and to others alienated or marginalized in the Church. There were stories about his own struggles with alcohol and his recovery with the help of Alcoholics Anonymous, and stories of his love for the firefighters, his courage in joining them on the front lines, his support as they coped with stress and sorrow. There seemed to be special meaning in the fact that Fr. Mychal was listed as the first certified casualty of 9/11.

A photograph of his fellow firemen carrying his body from the wreckage to a neighboring church became an icon of that day: an image of loving service and sacrifice, a hopeful answer to messages born of fear and fanaticism.

God is not an obligation or a burden.

God is the joy of my life!

—Fr. Mychal Judge

SISTER DOROTHY HENNESSEY
Franciscan, Witness for Peace
(1913–2008)
· · · · · · · · ·

In 2001, Sr. Dorothy Hennessey, eighty-eight, made headlines when she was arrested with her younger sister Gwen Hennessey for trespassing at the School of the Americas in Fort Benning, Georgia. They were part of a large contingent of human rights protesters waging a campaign to close the school, whose alumni included the perpetrators of torture, massacres, and military coups in Latin America. Dorothy and Gwen were sentenced to six months in prison. When their judge offered to commute Dorothy's sentence to "motherhouse arrest," she replied, "I'd rather not be singled out. If you wouldn't mind, I would just as soon have the same sentence as the others."

Dorothy had entered the Franciscan order at nineteen and spent many years teaching. But over time, her sense of global responsibility was awakened through letters from her brother Ron Hennessey, a Maryknoll priest in Guatemala, who reported on the violence and atrocities occurring at the hands of the military. In the early 1980s she went to Nicaragua during the time of the Contra war to serve as a witness for peace. In 1986, in her seventies, she took part in a continental walk for peace across the entire United States.

In 2002 she and her sister Gwen received the Pacem in Terris award from the diocese of Davenport, an award previously won by Mother Teresa, Dorothy Day, and Martin Luther King Jr. Dorothy died on January 24, 2008, at the age of ninety-four. Tom Harkin, senator from Iowa, entered into the *Congressional Record* these words from an article in the *Des Moines Register:* "Sister Hennessey taught many things, including courage, compassion, and the importance of independent thought and creative action. She taught that aging gracefully can be consistent with living meaningfully and even dangerously. But most important, she taught that we don't have to stand by in frustration when wrongs are perpetrated, even by our government; that the world is best served when we stand up for what is right. And that you do whatever you can, from wherever you are. In her case it was the Lord's work."

We can't protest everything, but we can pick out some of the worst things to protest, and that's what I've tried to do.

—Sr. Dorothy Hennessey

ᘓᘏ ⚜ ᘒᘌ

CALENDAR OF FEAST DAYS

JANUARY

4   St. Angela of Foligno (1248–1309)

6   St. Berard and Companions (d. 1220)

14   Blessed Odoric of Pordenone (ca. 1285–1331)

20   St. Bernard of Corleone (1605–1667)

23   St. Marianne Cope (1838–1918)

24   Sr. Dorothy Hennessey (1913–2008)

27   St. Angela Merici (1474–1540)

28   Servant of God Brother Juniper (d. 1258)

FEBRUARY

1   Blessed Verdiana (1182–1242)

4   St. Joan of Valois (1464–1505)

6   Blessed Maria Theresia Bonzel (1830–1905)
    Venerable Marthe Robin (1902–1981)

8   Blessed Jacoba of Settesoli (1190–1273)

10   St. Conrad of Piacenza (ca. 1290–1351)
    Fr. Daniel Egan (1915–2000)

22   St. Margaret of Cortona (1247–1297)

23   St. Isabel of France (1225–1270)

27   Blessed Caritas Brader (1860–1943)

MARCH

2   St. Agnes of Bohemia (1203–1280)

9   St. Catherine of Bologna (1413–1463)

12   Blessed Angela Salawa (1881–1922)

13 Blessed Dulce Pontes (1914–1992)

16 St. Colette (1381–1447)

29 Blessed Joan Mary de Maille (1332–1414)

30 Sr. Thea Bowman (1937–1990)

APRIL

2 St. Francis of Paola (1416–1507)

4 St. Benedict the Black (ca. 1526–1589)

5 St. Mary Crescentia (1682–1744)

7 Blessed Maria Assunta Pallotta (1878–1905)

9 St. Peter of Alcántara (1499–1562)

15 Mother Lurana White (1870–1935)

16 St. Benedict Joseph Labre (1748–1783)

23 Blessed Giles of Assisi (1190–1262)

24 St. Fidelis of Sigmaringen (1577–1622)

25 St. Pedro de San José Betancur (1619–1667)

27 St. Zita (1218–1278)

28 Blessed Luchesio and Buonadonna (d. 1260)

MAY

6 Blessed Mary Catherine of Cairo (1813–1887)
   Mother Mary Ignatius Hayes (1823–1894)

7 Blessed Anna Rosa Gattorno (1831–1900)

11 St. Ignatius of Laconi (1700–1781)

17 St. Paschal Baylon (1540–1592)

18 St. Felix of Cantalice (1515–1587)

21 Blessed Franz Jägerstätter (1907–1943)

24 Blessed John of Prado (d. ca. 1631)
   Venerable Maria of Jesus of Agreda (1602–1665)

26 St. Mariana of Quito (1618–1645)
31 St. Baptista Varano (1458–1524)
    Blessed Mariano Roccacasale (1778–1866)

JUNE
7   Blessed Humiliana of Cerchi (1219–1246)
13 St. Anthony of Padua (1195–1231)
20 Blessed Michelina of Pesaro (1300–1356)
22 St. Thomas More (1478–1535)
30 Blessed Ramón Lull (1232–1316)
    Mother Mary Bachmann (1824–1863)

JULY
1   St. Junipero Serra (1748–1783)
8   St. Elizabeth of Portugal (1271–1336)
9   Angelus Silesius (1624–1677)
    St. Veronica Giuliani (1660–1727)
    St. Hermina Grivot (1866–1900)
    Blessed Marija Petkovic (1892–1966)
10 Eve Lavalliere (1866–1929)
13 St. Francis Solano (1549–1610)
    St. Clelia Barbieri (1847–1870)
14 St. Bonaventure (1221–1274)
    Mother Theodore Williams (1868–1931)
16 St. Mary-Magdalen Postel (1756–1846)
24 St. Kunigunde of Poland (ca. 1224–1292)
    Blessed Louisa of Savoy (1461–1503)
27 Blessed Angelina of Marsciano (ca. 1377–1435)
31 Blessed Solanus Casey (1870–1957)

AUGUST

6   Venerable Antonio Margil (1657–1726)
9   Martyrs of Chimbote (d. 1991)
11   St. Clare (1194–1253)
13   St. Benedetto Sinigardi (1190–1282)
14   St. Maximilian Kolbe (1894–1941)
17   St. Roch (ca. 1348– ca. 1378)
18   Venerable Mary Magdalen Bentivoglio (1834–1905)
20   St. Louis of Anjou (1274–1297)
25   Blessed María del Tránsito Cabanillas (1821–1885)

SEPTEMBER

4   St. Rose of Viterbo (1235–1252)
11   Fr. Mychal Judge (1933–2001)
13   Dante Alighieri (1265–1321)
18   St. Joseph of Cupertino (1603–1663)
23   St. Pio of Pietrelcina (Padre Pio) (1887–1968)

OCTOBER

4   St. Francis of Assisi (1182–1226)
8   St. Birgitta of Sweden (1303–1373
11   St. John XXIII (1881–1963)
17   Blessed Contardo Ferrini (1959–1902)
22   Blessed John Baptist Bullaker (1604–1642)
29   Blessed Restituta Kafka (1894–1943)
31   Louis Massignon (1883–1962)

NOVEMBER

8   Blessed John Duns Scotus (ca. 1266–1308)

15 Blessed Mary of the Passion (1839–1904)

16 St. Agnes of Assisi (1197–1253)

19 St. Elizabeth of Hungary (1207–1231)

24 Venerable Margaret Sinclair (1900–1925)

25 St. Leonard of Port Maurice (1676–1751)

DECEMBER

7 St. Maria Josepha Rossello (1811–1880)

10 Servant of God Bernard of Quintavalle (d. ca. 1241)

18 Blessed Frances Schervier (1819–1876)

25 Blessed Jacopone of Todi (1230–1306)

ABOUT THE AUTHOR

Robert Ellsberg is the publisher and editor-in-chief of Orbis Books. He has written numerous books on saints, including *All Saints: Daily Reflections on Saints, Prophets, and Witnesses for Our Times*, *Blessed Among All Women*, *The Saints' Guide to Happiness*, *Modern Spiritual Masters*, and *Blessed Among Us: Day by Day with Saintly Witnesses*, which is based on his daily entries for *Give Us This Day*. A former managing editor of *The Catholic Worker*, he has written extensively about the life and legacy of Dorothy Day, and has also edited anthologies of writings by Gandhi, Flannery O'Connor, Thich Nhat Hanh, Charles de Foucauld, and Carlo Carretto, among others.